For Bill Daniel
With best wishes
JRvNPrice

Cane River Country Louisiana

~

Carol Wells
History and Copy Editor

Ezra Adams
Designer

Don Sepulvado
Photography Consultant

~

Northwestern State University Press

Natchitoches, Louisiana

1979

Published with funds
from the John S. Kyser Endowment
and the
Northwestern State University Foundation

Copyright © 1979
by the
Northwestern State University Press.

All rights reserved

Manufactured
in the
United States of America

Type face: Caledonia
Printer: Taylor Publishing Company
Binder: Taylor Publishing Company

Library of Congress Catalog
Card Number 79-66631

ISBN 0-917898-03-6

Foreword

CANE RIVER COUNTRY Louisiana is a story about a people and their landscape, legacy, and history. This book is also a commentary on a community and its affection for a university — Northwestern State University. While there is much in this volume about the beauty of our landscape, our people and their lives, there is much of "The Old Normal," the "Louisiana State Normal College," "Northwestern State College," and "Northwestern State University" in this volume, too. The university is portrayed as it was at many different times, because our people have long, long memories.

Community and alumni fondness for Northwestern was not lost on our university, because one of the first publications planned by the NSU Press was a pictorial history of the Cane River area. We at the university were also concerned about preserving the history and culture of the Cane River country before certain aspects of it were lost forever — many buildings and homes pictured in these pages have already been destroyed. The catalyst that pushed us toward a commitment to do this book *now* was the proposal made to our university by Mrs. John S. Kyser, widow of the late Dr. John S. Kyser, a former president of our university. Mrs. Kyser had attended planning meetings for this and other publications projected by the university press. The recently established NSU Press needed financial support, and Mrs. Kyser felt that an appropriate memorial to Dr. John Kyser would be an endowment to the NSU Press.

The Kyser endowment was made directly to help establish a fund for publishing books — especially to help with a book that "the community needed and wanted" — about Cane River country. On behalf of Northwestern State University I would like to thank both Mrs. John S. Kyser and her daughter Janet Kyser for their interest in and love for our university. This book is a memorial to John S. Kyser, a pioneer in Louisiana's audio-visual program who believed that a "picture is worth a thousand words."

René J. Bienvenu, President
Northwestern State University

Courtesy B. A. Cohen

CANE RIVER COUNTRY Louisiana — iii

HENRI DE TONTI

On Feb. 17, 1690, Henri de Tonti, a trader and French army officer known as the Iron Hand, arrived in this area to search for La Salle's lost colony. While here, he helped arrange a treaty between the Taensa and Natchitoches Indians.

ERECTED BY THE LOUISIANA TOURIST DEVELOPMENT COMMISSION, 1965

Courtesy B. A. Cohen

Introduction

CANE RIVER COUNTRY Louisiana is a long-awaited book. For the past several years many people in the Natchitoches area discussed the need for a pictorial history of the Cane River country. The community was aware of rare photographs in the archival collections at Northwestern State University. Also, many individuals in the area had photographs of events, houses, and persons long gone. So *CANE RIVER COUNTRY Louisiana* is several things: it is a long-awaited pictorial history; it is a gathering together of glimpses of bygone years, places, and events; it is a collection of various facets of the beauty of our natural landscape as it exists; it is a survey of the Natchitoches Historic District and the plantations along the Cane; lastly it is a labor of love on the part of our university, the alumni, and the Cane River community.

Certain explanatory remarks are in order about the scope and guidelines followed in doing this book. The NSU Press Board held public meetings with Natchitoches people and the consensus was that no living or readily identifiable person would be included in the volume. New homes were not included unless they were in the Historic District, and not all worthy homes, new or old, could be included. Likewise, the "boundaries" of the book include Natchitoches Parish and adjacent important historical areas like Fort Jesup and St. Maurice. Wherever possible homes are identified as owners wished, or traditional historic designations are used. Although some photographs or maps were not of good reproduction quality they were the only copies available and were included because of their importance. The NSU Press tried diligently to identify each item as correctly as possible. The public was invited to contribute their photographs and ideas for the book and every idea and item was appreciated and evaluated. The theme of *CANE RIVER COUNTRY Louisiana* is more of a *potpourri* approach than topical, subject, or even chronological. It was agreed that the surprise, delight, and curiosity achieved by the juxtaposition of unassociated pictures and text would be best for this volume. Possibly subsequent volumes might be arranged according to themes: architecture, people, history, geography, and so on.

The narrative for this book is drawn from local authors, writers, and historians. In most cases the narrative gives the reader a perspective of those persons contemporary with the pictures with which it is associated. In other words, contemporaries of the times do the narration.

Many people contributed to this book. The direct contributions are noted in the credit lines under the illustrations. The most important persons are those who contributed their photographs or other items with permission to use them.

The following individuals helped personally or professionally during various publishing stages: Jerri Adams, Bobbie Archibald, Joy Nell Bailey, Catherine Bienvenu, Clyde Bostick, Judy Boyd, Bob Burk, Lucille Carnahan, Alvin DeBlieux, Sharon Gahagan, James Hearron, Jim Johnson, Betty Jones, Juanita Kilpatrick, Thelma Kyser, Laura Lavespere, Sudie Lawton, Mildred Lee, Walter Ledet, Mildred McCoy, Theodosia Nolan, Jerry Pierce, Faye Price, Lucille Prudhomme, Mike Sibley, Sylvan Sibley, Robert Smith, Evelyne Taylor, Lovan Thomas, Pat Thomas, Peter Wells, Dixie Whittington, and Irma Sompayrac Willard.

Robert DeBlieux is due a special thanks not only for contributing photographs but also for spending several hours helping the NSU Press staff locate hard-to-find photographs, and helping to identify many scenes and buildings. His knowledge of local history and architecture proved invaluable.

Also, Tommy Johnson for making his entire slide collection available and for spending many hours selecting slides and identifying places and subjects. Ed Dranguet not only served on the NSU Press Board but also helped in many other ways when needed. Other members of the NSU Press Board — Dr. René Bienvenu, Dr. Thomas P. Southerland, Dr. Bennie Barron, Dr. Otis Cox, Dr. Mary Dell Fletcher, Dr. Mildred H. Bailey, Dr. Edward W. Graham, Dr. William B. Knipmeyer, Dr. Robert Palmatier, Dr. Donald M. Rawson, and Dr. George A. Stokes were patient and encouraged the project at all stages. The Service League of Natchitoches Inc. is due special recognition for their faith in the project as well as special permission to include photographs from *Cane River Cuisine*. The Natchitoches Parish Chamber of Commerce and the Association for the Preservation of Historic Natchitoches helped promote the book. Guillet Photography and especially John C. Guillet did special color processing for the book and also gave permission for us to use his collection of valuable negatives. We greatly profited from his experience and knowledge in photography. Mary Carolyn Roberts did watercolors especially for this book — they speak for themselves.

Of all the acknowledgements, two individuals stand out for their contributions. One is Barbara Anne Cohen, who spent several weeks doing special photography. She met with the NSU Press staff numerous times, spent long hours on the book, and constantly encouraged the project. She did all this at her own time and expense. Without her help it would not have been possible to publish at this time. The other individual who has worked so hard for the NSU Press and has done so much not only for this book but also for other NSU Press books is Donald MacKenzie, director of the NSU Library. When the NSU Press was organized he provided office space and supplies during its first year of existence. Besides that, he lent his unselfish personal help and encouragement as well as that of his office staff. His help, support, and understanding have been very important in this endeavor.

Lastly, the three NSU staff people whose names appear on the title page pulled the book together and gave real life to it: Carol Wells did an excellent job on the copy and historical editing; Ezra Adams created the layout and design, and Don Sepulvado was an outstanding photography consultant. Their efforts produced an extraordinary job and one of which we can be proud.

John Price
Director, NSU Press

Courtesy B. A. Cohen

Fort St. Jean Baptiste des Natchitoches

Courtesy of Don Sepulvado

Journal of Official Acts, Post of Natchitoches: Two-page entry showing the transfer of the post and archives

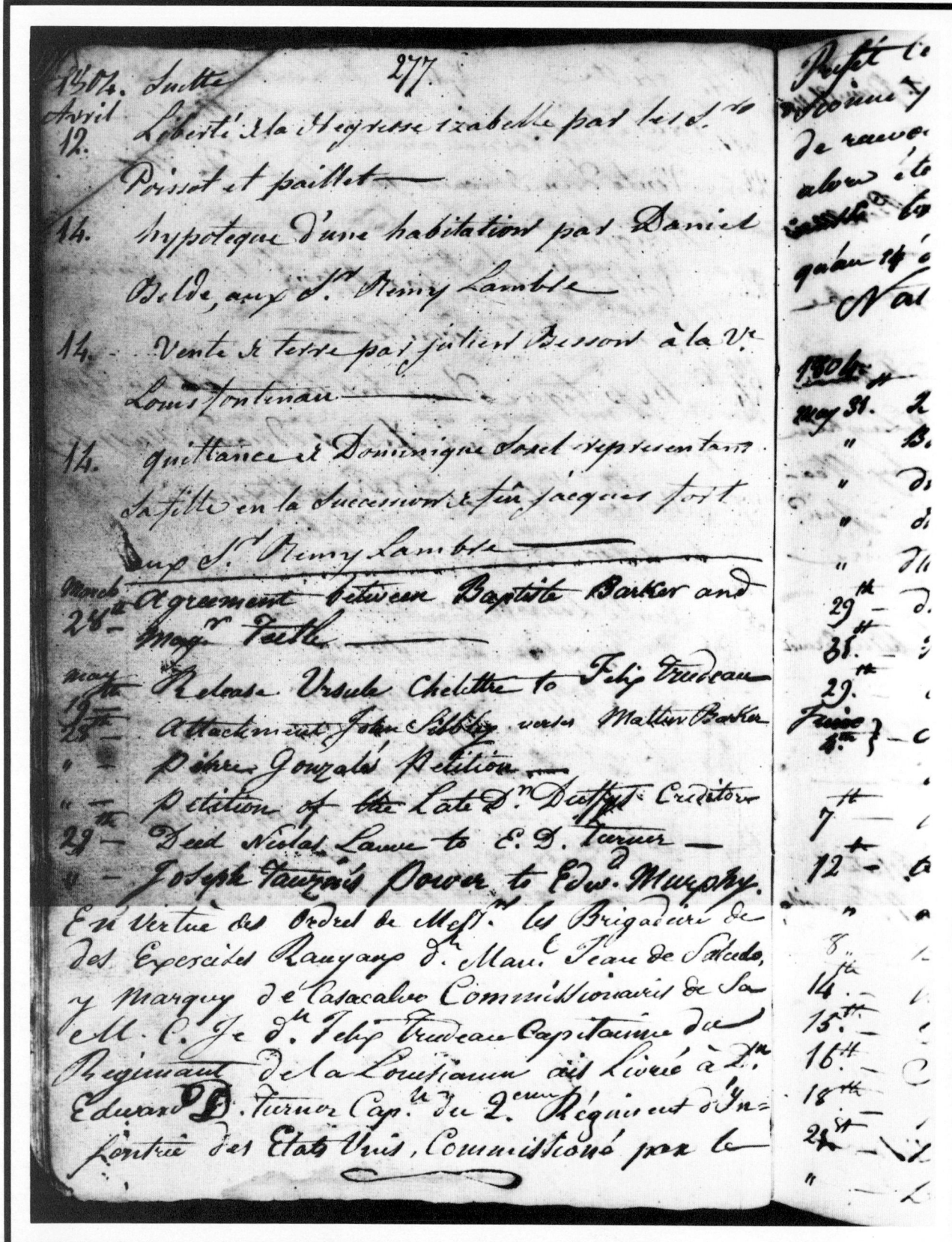

Melrose Collection, NSU Archives

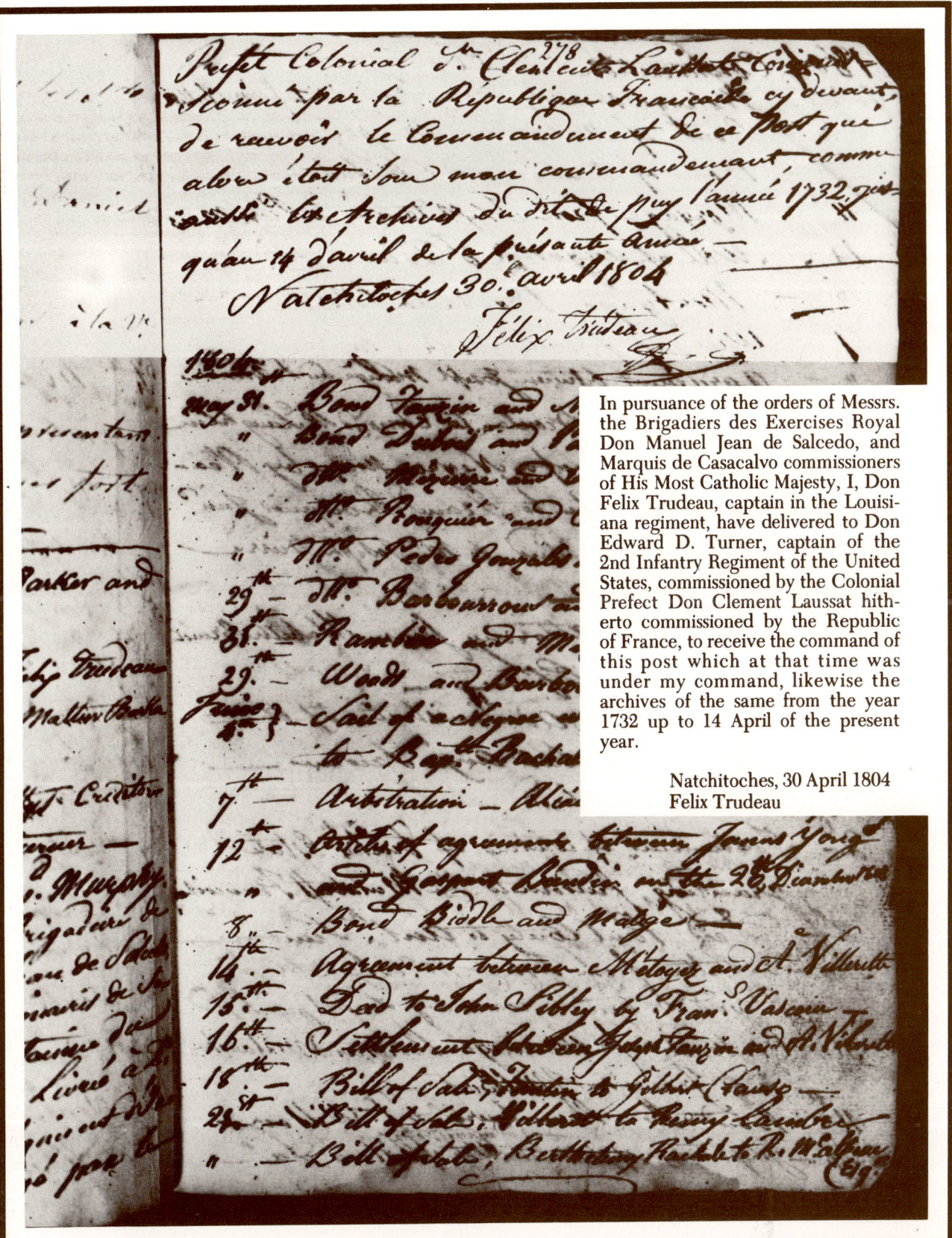

In pursuance of the orders of Messrs. the Brigadiers des Exercises Royal Don Manuel Jean de Salcedo, and Marquis de Casacalvo commissioners of His Most Catholic Majesty, I, Don Felix Trudeau, captain in the Louisiana regiment, have delivered to Don Edward D. Turner, captain of the 2nd Infantry Regiment of the United States, commissioned by the Colonial Prefect Don Clement Laussat hitherto commissioned by the Republic of France, to receive the command of this post which at that time was under my command, likewise the archives of the same from the year 1732 up to 14 April of the present year.

Natchitoches, 30 April 1804
Felix Trudeau

Melrose Collection, NSU Archives

CANE RIVER COUNTRY Louisiana — 3

A little further up, but on the West bank, the Red river empties into the Mississippi. Thirty leagues from its mouth, on the lands of the Natchitoches, the French on their arrival in Louisiana erected a few palisade [type structures]. This post had as its purpose the taking from New Mexico of fur-bearing and horned animals which a growing colony always needs, and of opening clandestine commerce with the Spanish fort of Adayes which is only seven leagues away. The natural growth of open-stock herds in the countryside soon put an end to the first plan, and the second purpose had been concluded with one of the poorest establishments in the world that will never have any real development. Natchitoches was speedily abandoned by those who aspired to fame and fortune. The only ones who stayed were descendants of a few soldiers who were stationed there at the end of their enlistments. Their number was never over two hundred. They lived on the maize or beans they grew, and they sold the surplus to their indolent neighbors. The money they derived from that weak garrison served to pay for their drinks and even for the clothing which they were obliged to get from elsewhere.
    G. T. Raynal, *Histoire Philosophique et Politique,* 1820

Certificate of honorable discharge of Jean Denis Buard and his son Gabriel Buard, signed by Captain François Louis De Merveilleux, and dated 1 May 1725

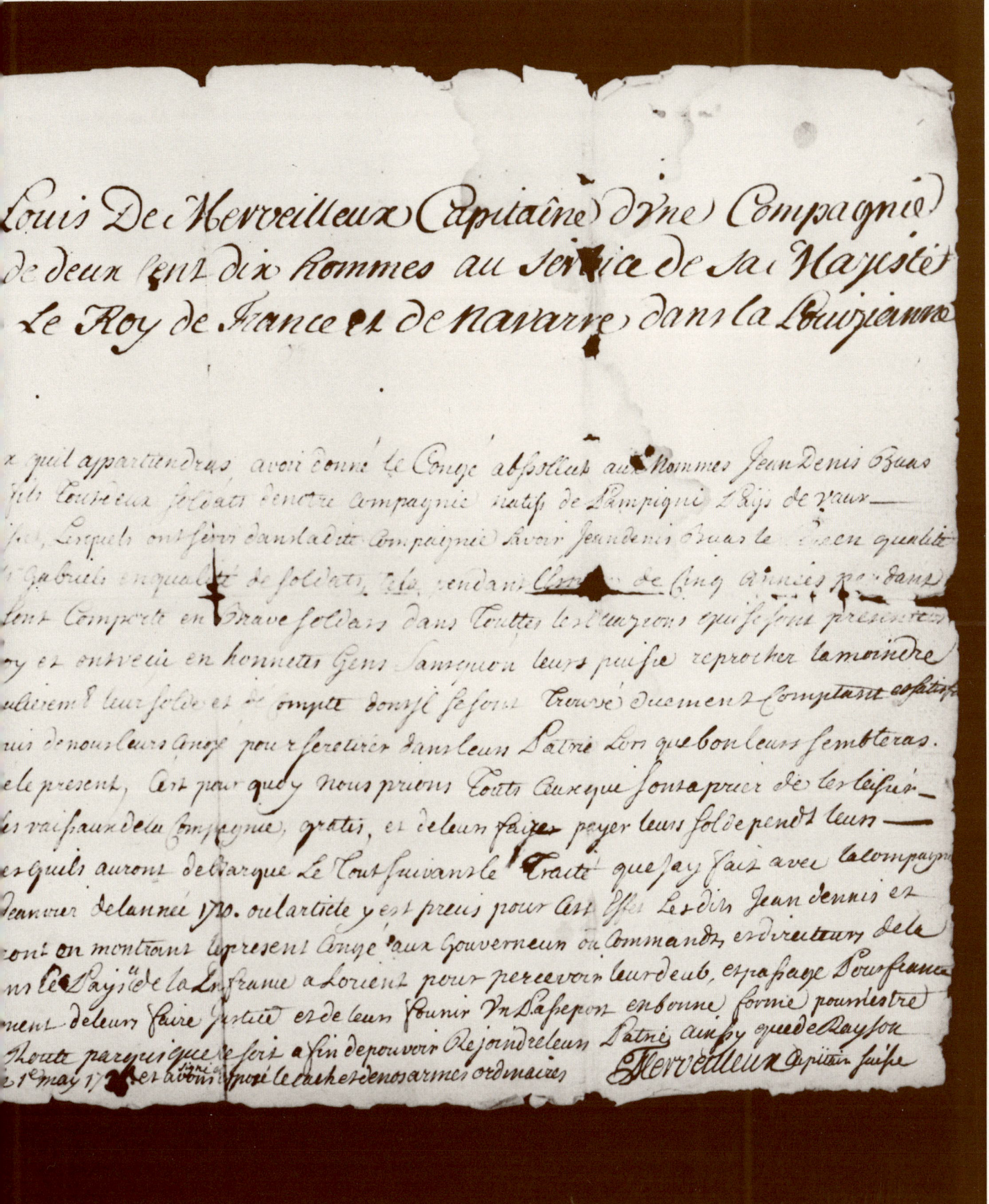

Peter Cloutier Collection, NSU Archives

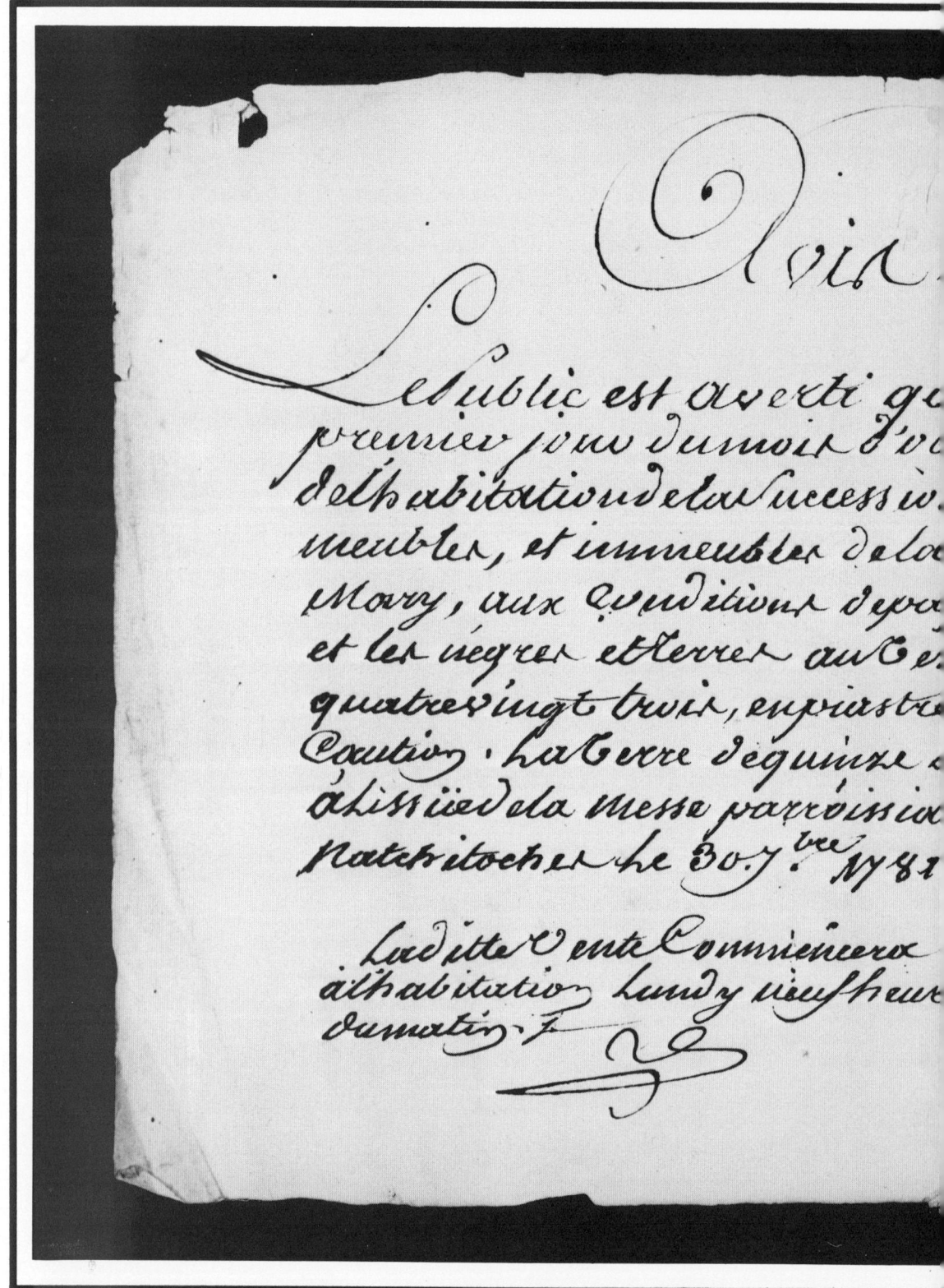

Notice of a public sale to take place at the residence of the late Mme. Poisot, to start at the conclusion of the Sunday, October first, mass at the royal fort; signed by Commandant Vaugine at the royal fort, Post of Natchitoches, 30 September 1781

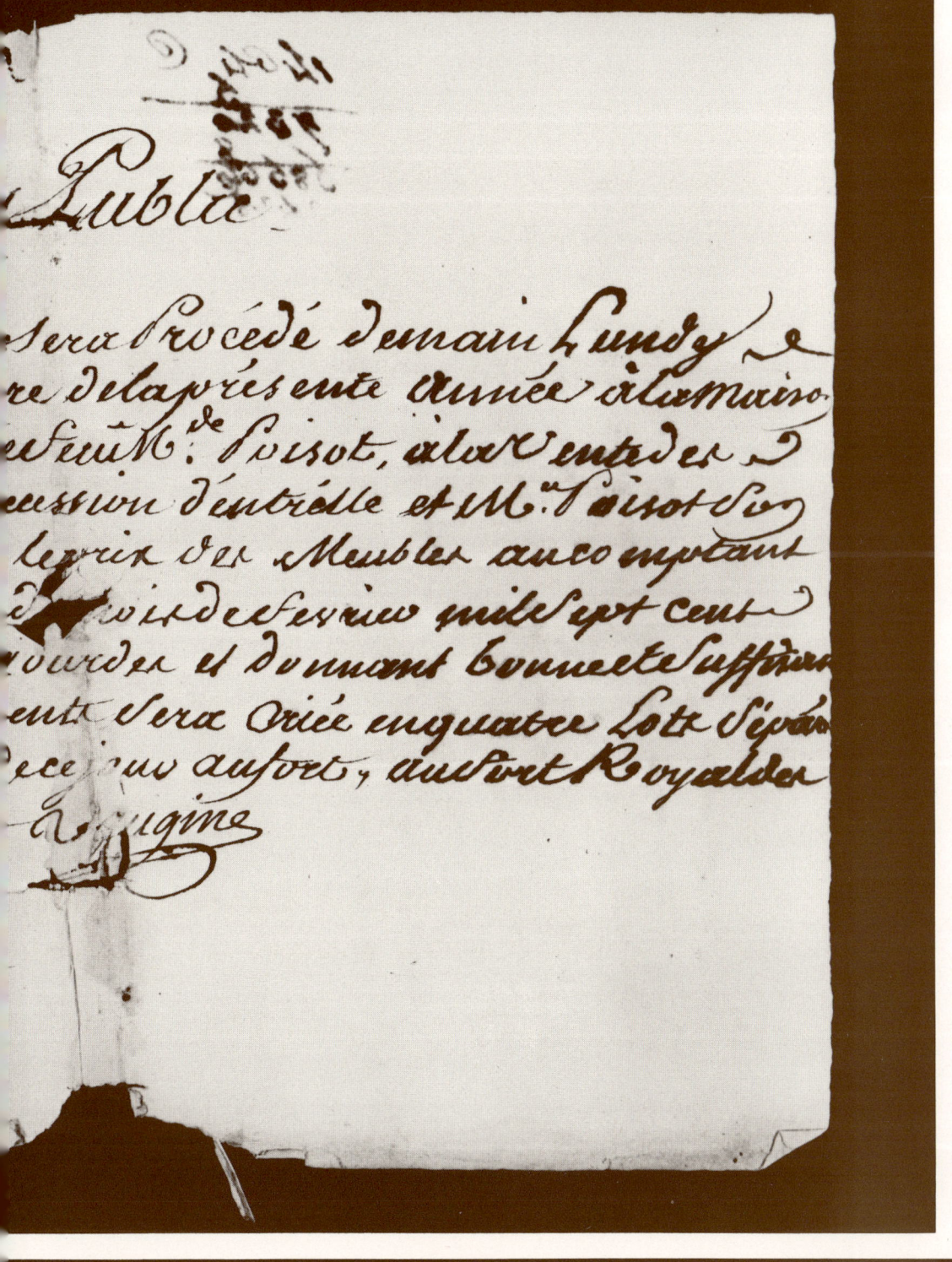

Melrose Collection, NSU Archives

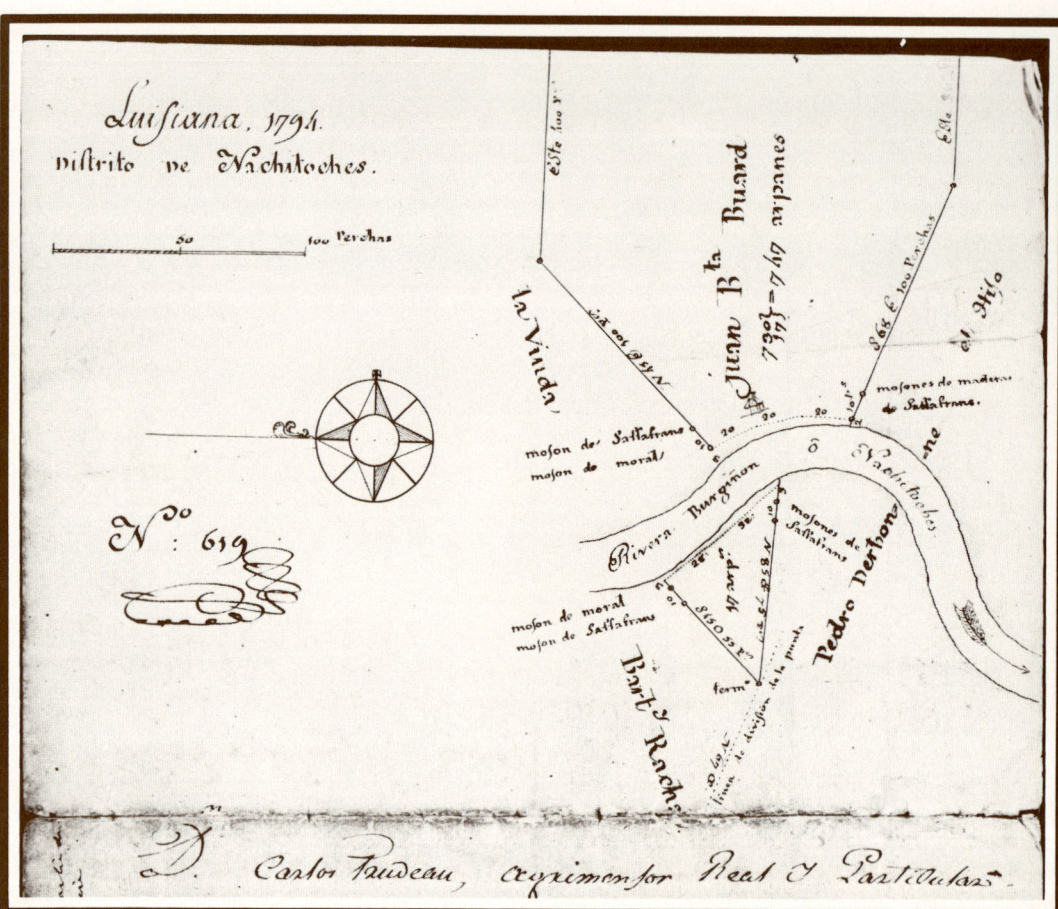

Peter Cloutier Collection, NSU Archives

1794: land of Juan Baptista Buard on the Rivera Burgiñon, bordered by lands of Pedro Derbon and son and the widow of Bartelemy Rachal

1795: land of Guillaume Lestage bordered by lands of Francisco Leconte and Luis Buard.

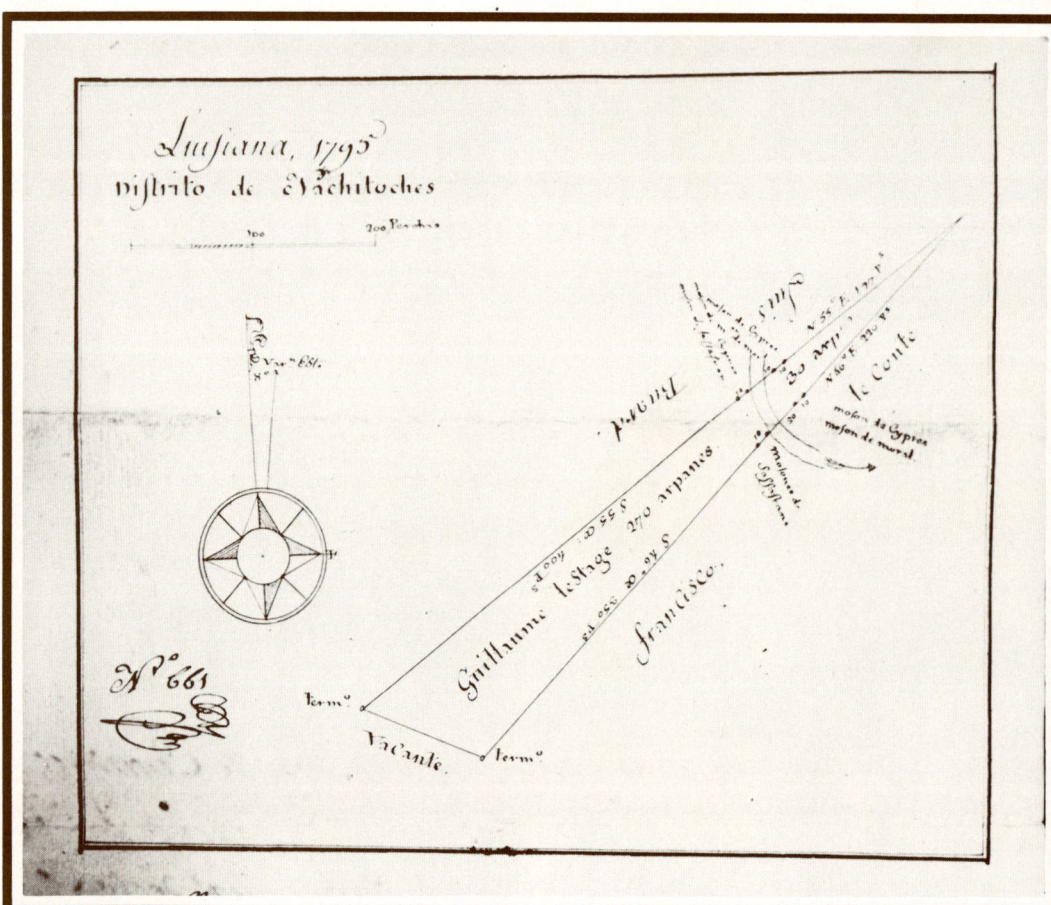

Peter Cloutier Collection, NSU Archives

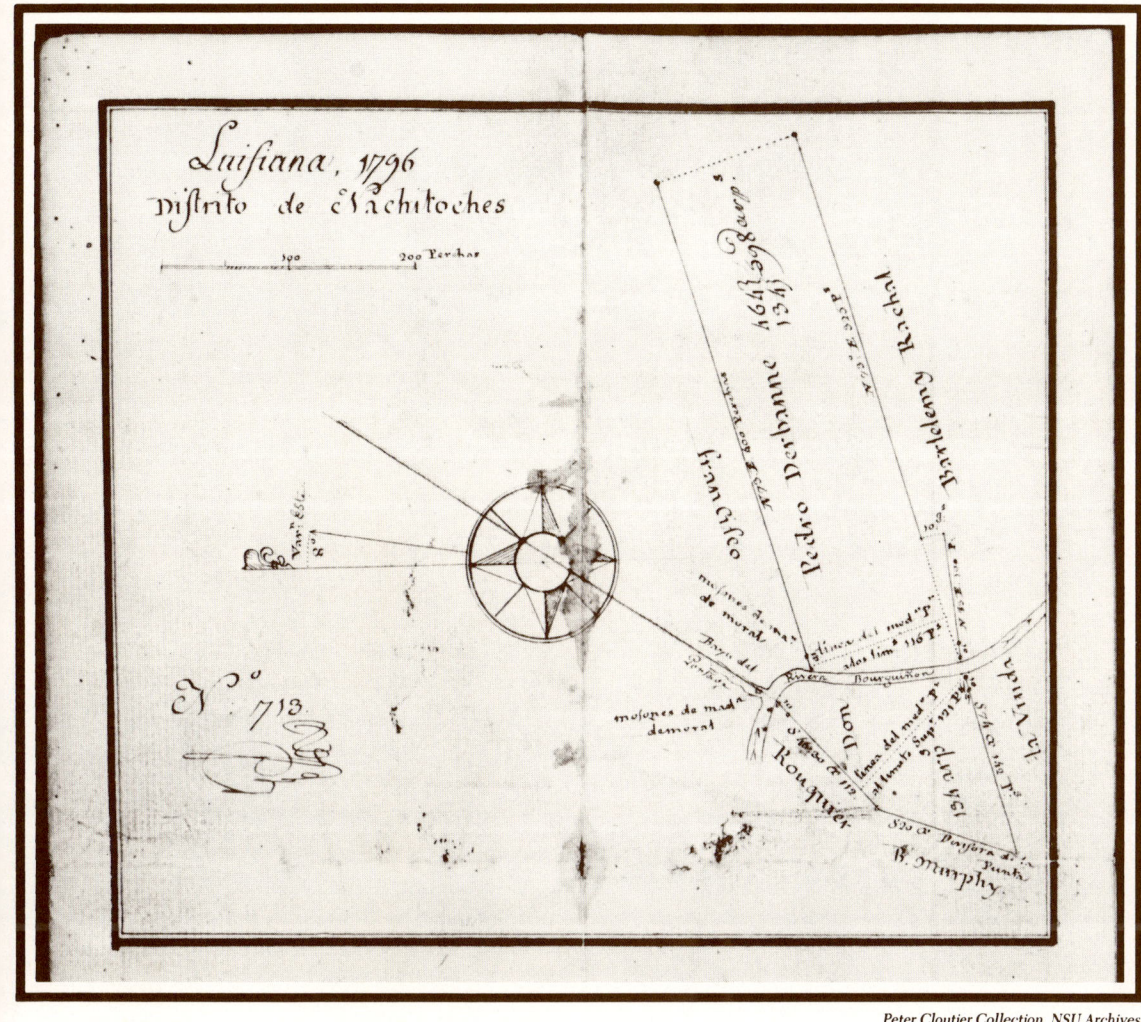

1796: land of Pedro Derbanne on Rivera Bourguiñon bordered by lands of the widow Bartelemy Rachal, B. Murphy, and Francisco Rouquier.

Peter Cloutier Collection, NSU Archives

From the rapids to Natchitoches, a distance of about one hundred and ten miles, the settlements are thinly scattered along the river, and most on the right bank of it. Nearly the whole of this tract, especially along the water courses, is composed of bottom land of the richest kind, and well covered with wood, though in some instances for the space of fifteen or twenty miles no settlements have been made. These, however, begin to be numerous and wealthy about thirty miles below Natchitoches, and they multiply as that place is approached. One great inconvenience is, that the bottom lands suitable for cultivation extend only in narrow borders along the river, generally from three hundred to four hundred yards in depth, and are bounded in the rear by cypress swamps and lakes. These swamps and lakes almost invariably extend parallel to the river, and are seldom more than one or two miles wide. They are bounded on the opposite side by the high lands which are of a rolling nature, interspersed with extensive rich prairies, and small ridges of pine and othe timber; and the lands of this mixed quality extend westward to the Sabine. Many elevated situations occur along the river, and back of it, which afford delightful views. From some of them the eye may glance over vast natural meadows, thickly studded with copses of trees, adorned with variegated herbage.

Amos Stoddard, *Sketches, Historical and Descriptive, of Louisiana,* 1812

Commission of John Nancarrow, Sheriff of Natchitoches County, 1806

George Williamson Collection, NSU Archives

Natchitoches, 4th January 1812
His Excellency Govr. Claiborne

The commission of robbers on the Territory West of the Arroyo Hondo, and East of the Sabine River, and as your memorialists believe within the limits of your Excellency's Government, has become so frequent, that it is no longer safe to travel on the highways & roads through which the commerce of this Parish with the adjoining Mexican provinces have hitherto been carried on ... on the 2nd of January Inst. a Company of Spaniards, whilst travelling on the highway leading from the Sabine to Bayou Pierre, were attacked by a party of Said Banditti about thirty in number, with their faces blacked, and otherwise disfigured, who fired upon them, killed one man, wounded several, one it is supposed mortally so, and robbed them of all their horses, mules, baggage and about six thousand dollars in specie ...

Compere & Hertzog, Vienne & Landray, C. Pavie & Ce., Jos. Tauzin, A. Sompayrac, Jn. Cortes, Ambse. Duval & Ete. Lauve.

The Territorial Papers of the United States, Vol. IX

Location of Fort Claiborne, 1808

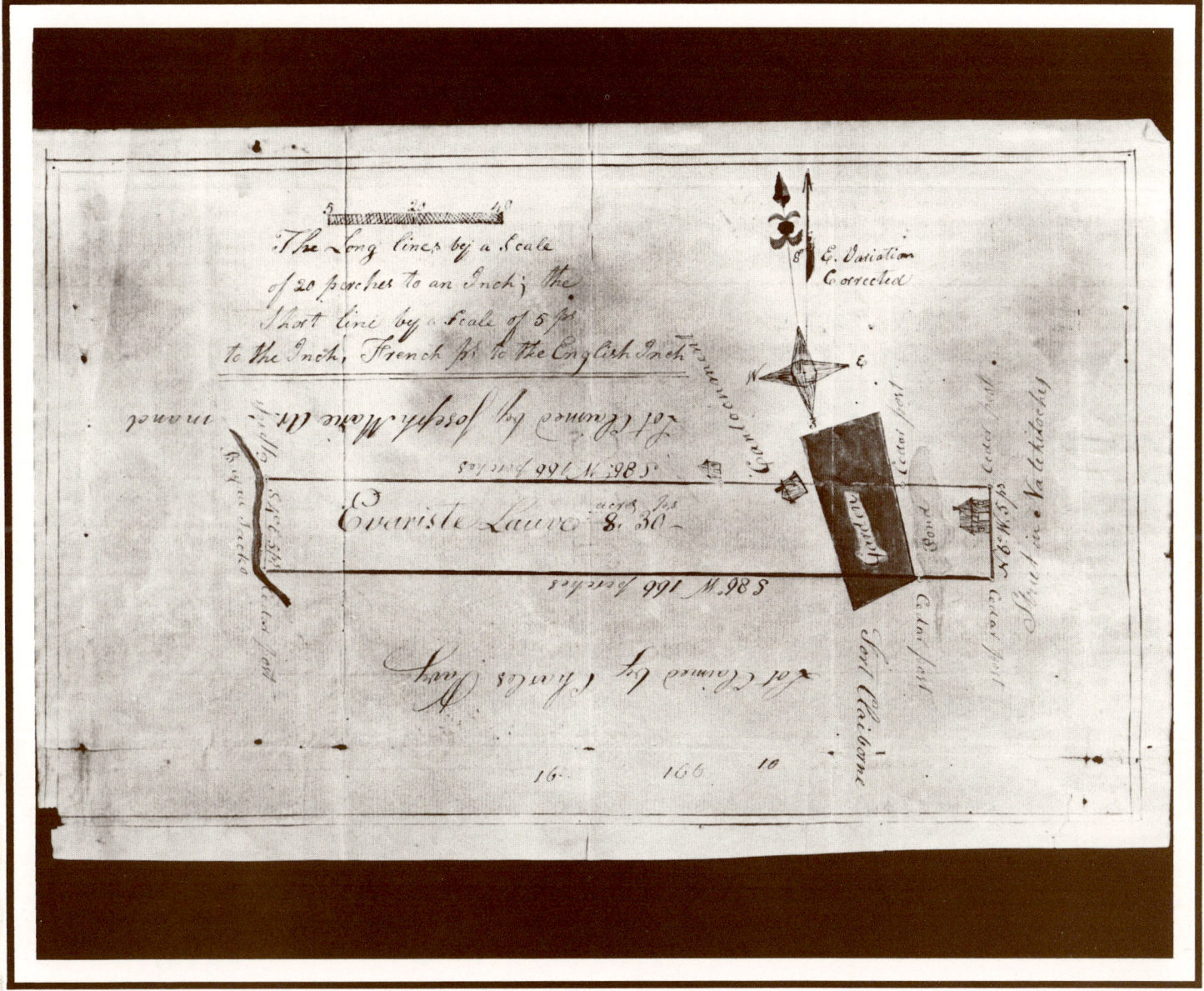

Hughes Collection, NSU Archives

Fort Claiborne, March 6, 1812

... The situation of the Garrison is much to be lamented, and is productive of a train of disadvantages easily foreseen by military men and alone to be remedied by one more eligible when speaking in a military point of view. It is commanded on the south and west by hills within Musket shot — It is nearly surrounded by a lagoon of Water which stands three fourths of the year productive of poisonous effluvia, and a host of musketoes — this lagoon alone separates it from the village, its proximity to which gives the soldier free scope to indulge himself in all the vices of the age, which is every way calculated to seduce him from his duty & ruins his health and dissipates his morality. — I now, Sir, approach the publick purse — The Buildings in toto want repairing — this will be productive of much labor and expense to the publick — and it must be done this summer, for the comfort and health of the Troops, it no longer can be delayed.

    Captain Walter H. Overton to Zebulon M. Pike
    The Territorial Papers of the United States: The Territory of Orleans, 1803-1812

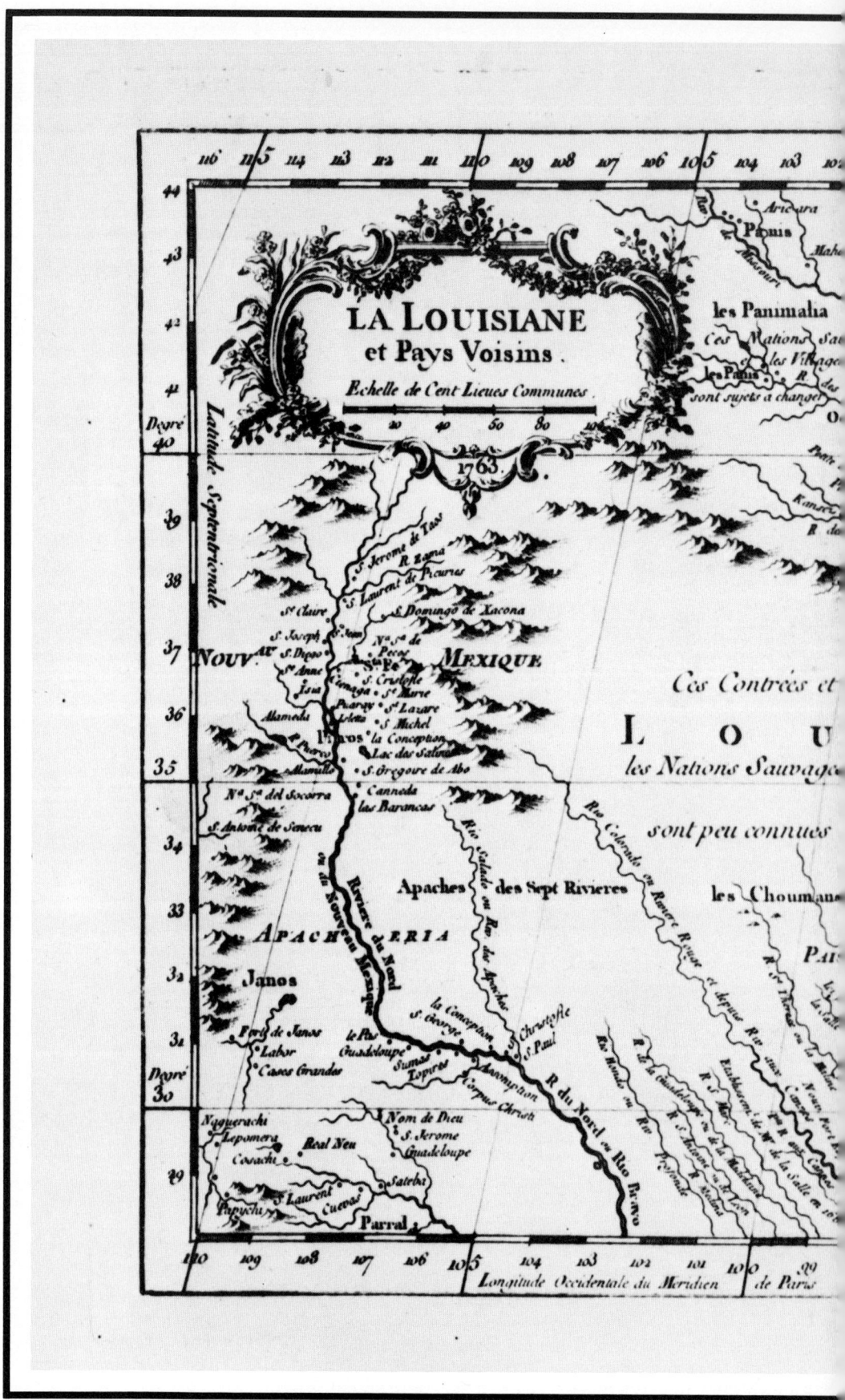

Louisiana and neighboring countries, undated map by Jacques Nicolas Bellin, c. 1764.

Map Collection, NSU Archives

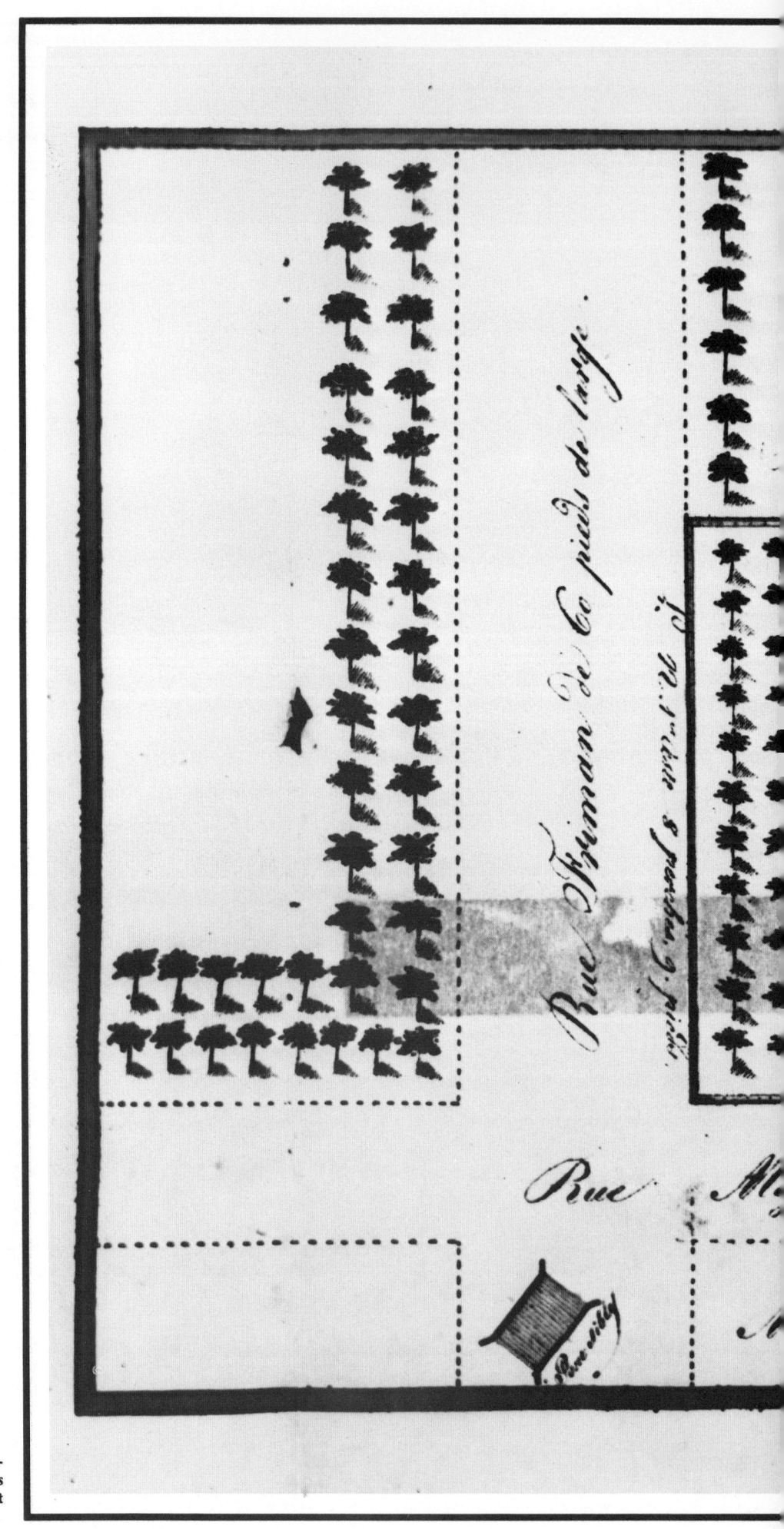

Sale of lot on Rue Mézière by John Baptiste Jacques Paillette and William Murray; the lot adjoins the lot of the Widow Chamard and the street called Rue Furman; 6 March 1810.

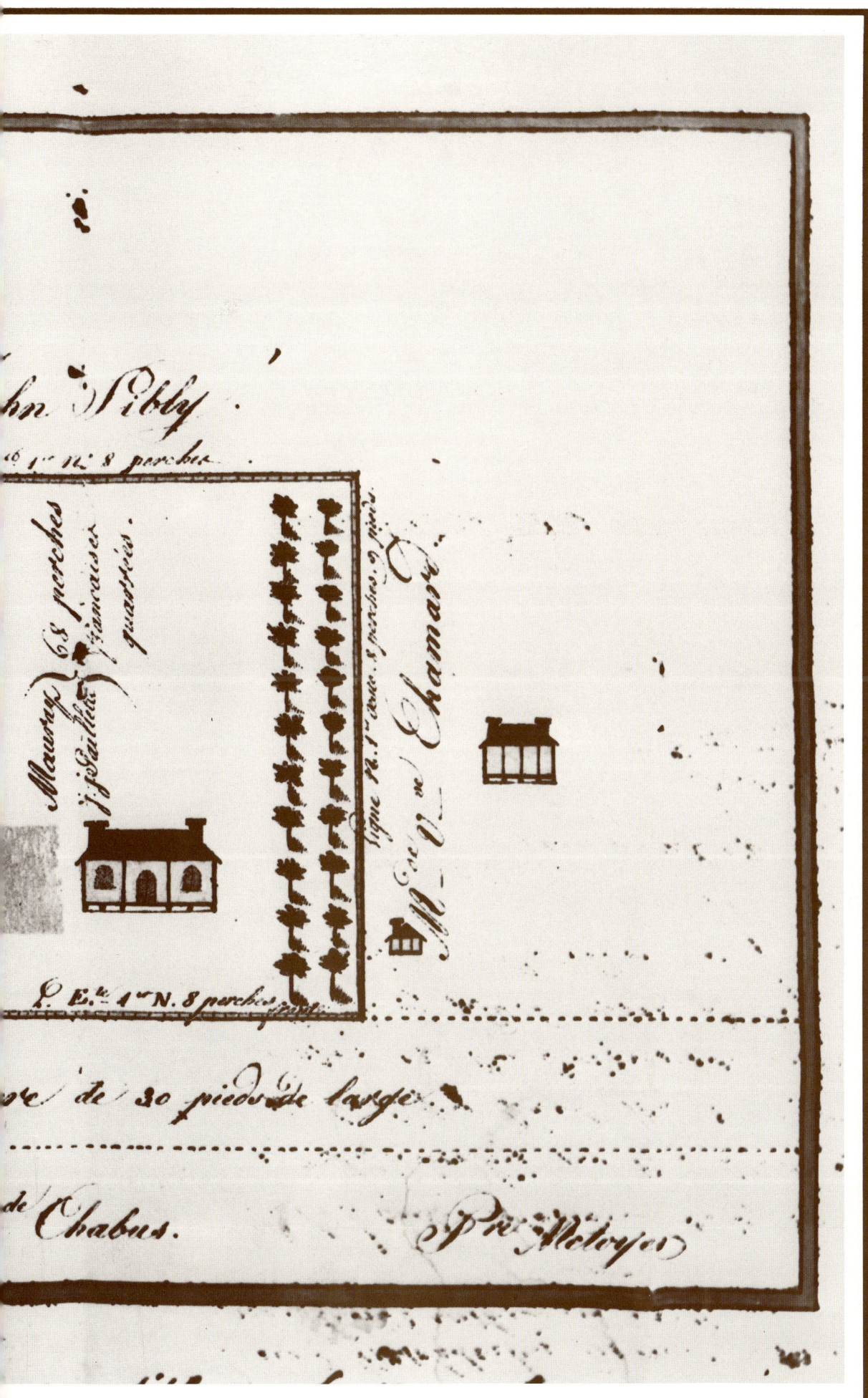

Peter Cloutier Collection, NSU Archives

Excerpts from letters St. Denis wrote to the Spanish governor, Don Manuel de Sandoval, when he objected to the French fort's being moved from an island in the river to a nearby hill:

> The land of Nachitoos has always been situated as it is today. There the river Colorado, or Rubro, flows from north to south. I have here on the east side the land of the French, who inhabit it. On the west is an island on which the French presidio was placed in the beginning, and on which it remained until the day of its removal. Between the two is the river itself. The said island most certainly belongs to the disputed land, because on its west side there is nothing except a flat hillock which, when the river is flooded, encloses a branch of it. When the latter is dry it is not extensive and does not form any obstacle. On the contrary, one travels without difficulty from the island to the disputed territory and to the site of the presidio.

⊕ ⊕ ⊕

> The French presidio never stood on the other side of the said river. It was always on this side, because in truth it had its beginnings in the camp of the Natchitoches Indians, and its existence on the island belonging to the disputed territory, unless the Spaniards may want to give the name of river to the branch of a river which becomes dry and which we have crossed in times past and we cross today without difficulty.

⊕ ⊕ ⊕

> I am removing our presidio only a stone's throw from the site where it formerly was. It is a place midway between

Broutin map of Natchitoches (1722 should be 1732).

16 — CANE RIVER COUNTRY Louisiana

R. Thomassy, Geologie Pratique de la Louisiane, *1859*

an adjoining lake and a branch of the river which becomes dry and which has been crossed and is being crossed today without difficulty.

If because of this branch of the river which becomes dry, it seems, or one judges, that the French are on the other side of the river, with how much more reason should they now also be considered so to be because of the lake that never goes dry and that receives the waters of the river when it is in flood, sometimes from the north and then again from the south?

◇◇◇

I am surprised and shall always be surprised that the right of the French to move their presidio a stone's throw is disputed. Who set boundaries between us and you? We are not taking your lands from you; leave us ours. Believe me that I do not act without orders. They are superior orders, but, presuming that there were none, I serve the Most Christian King. I must serve and look to the interests of my king . . .

August 22, 1736   Saint Denis

◇◇◇

All the above quotations are from *Pichardo's Treatise on the Limits of Louisiana and Texas,* 1941

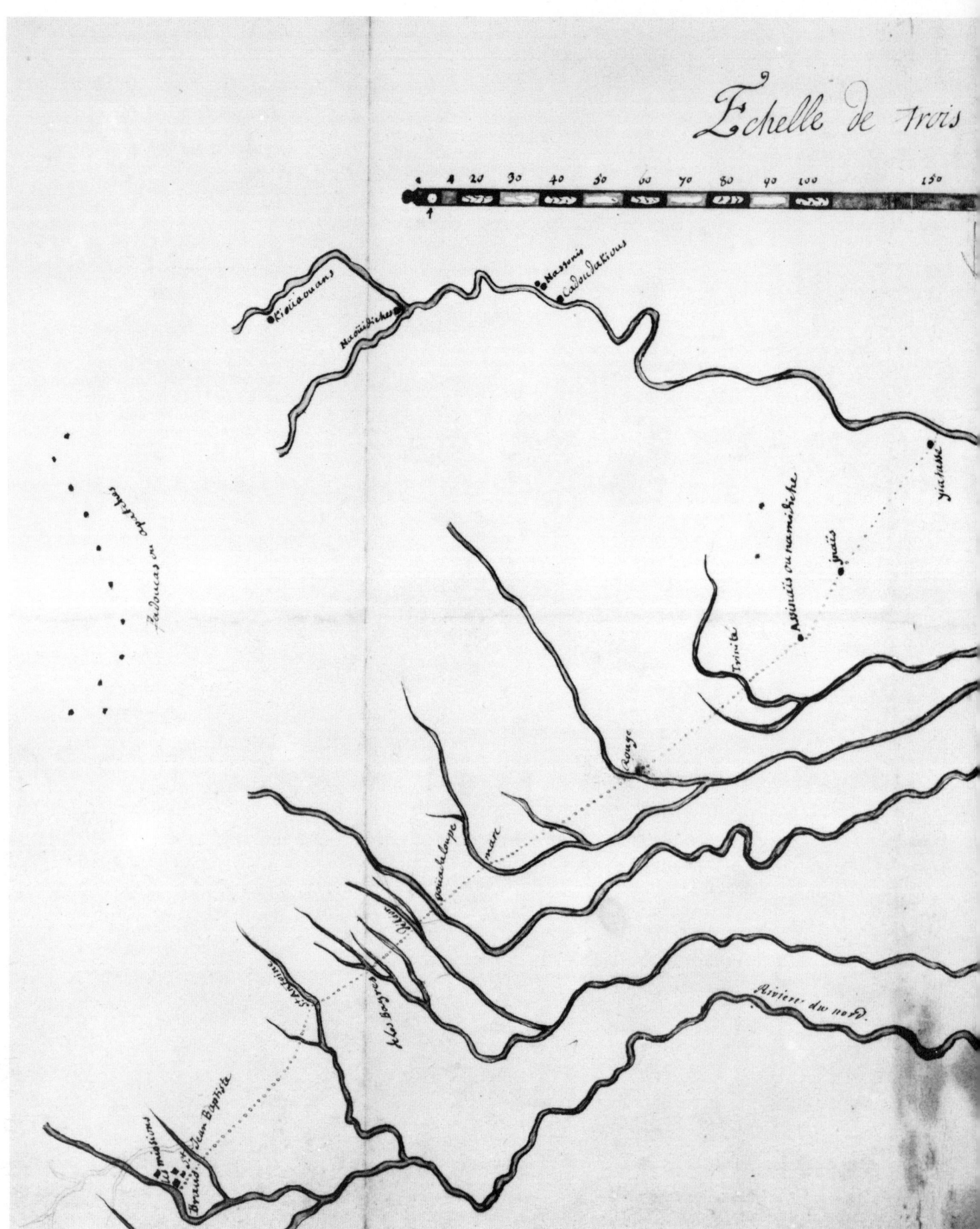

Undated map of Louisiana drawn prior to the founding of New Orleans. Unsigned.

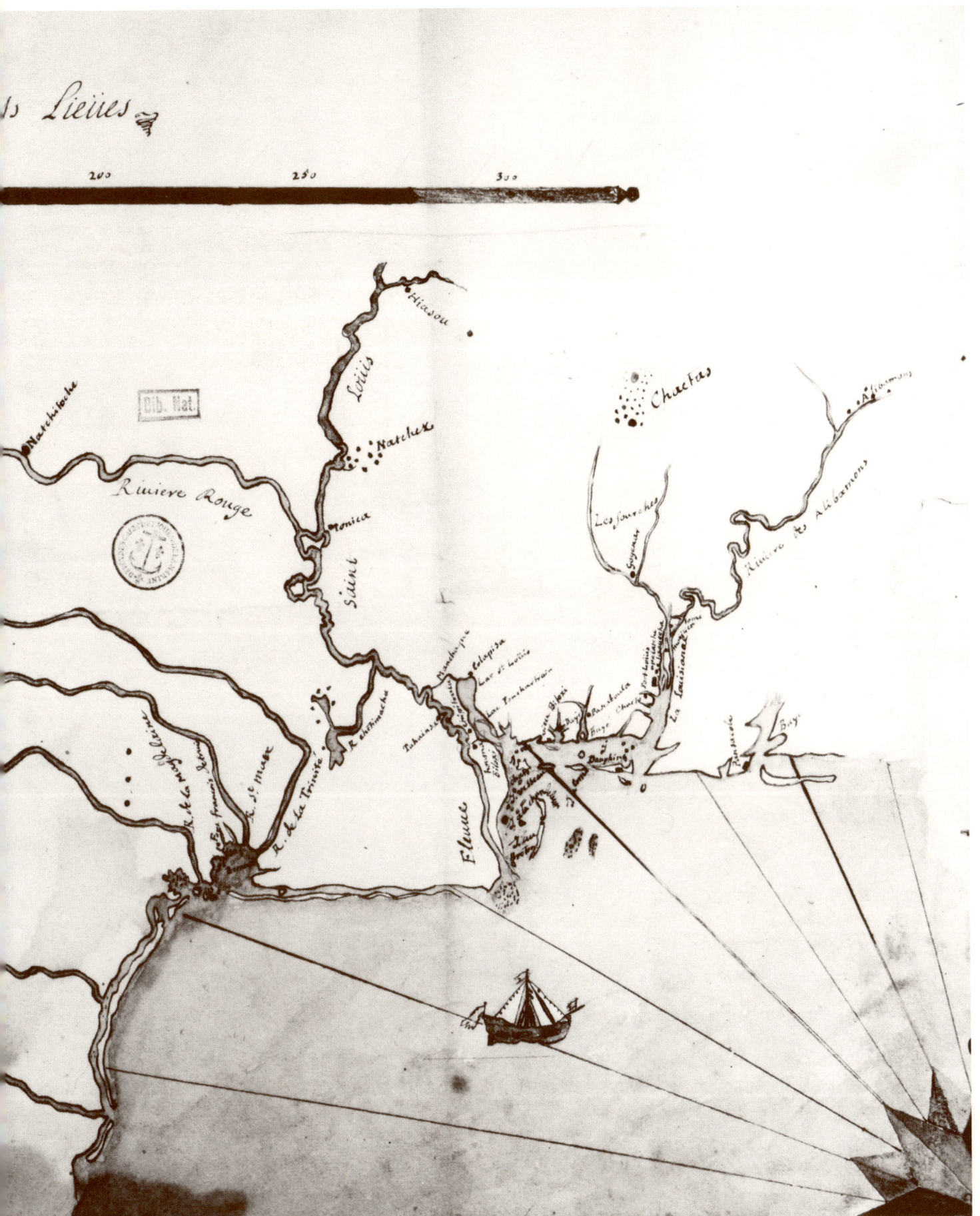
Bibliothèque National, Paris; courtesy Mrs. William Nolan

Photo from the Library of Congress, NSU Archives

Perhaps few travelers, who pass over the highway between Robeline and Natchitoches, La., ever realize that they have crossed what was once an international boundary, and come within hearing distance of the capital site of a province more vast than the largest of the present commonwealth of the United States.

Ross Phares,
Melrose Collection, NSU Archives

Photo from the British Museum in the NSU Archives

Rumors alone were their guides through a wild and desolate country;
Till, at the little inn of the Spanish town of Adayes,
Weary and worn, they alighted and learned from the garrulous landlord
That on the day before, with horses and guides and companions,
Gabriel left the village, and took the road of the prairies.
                Henry Wadsworth Longfellow, *Evangeline*

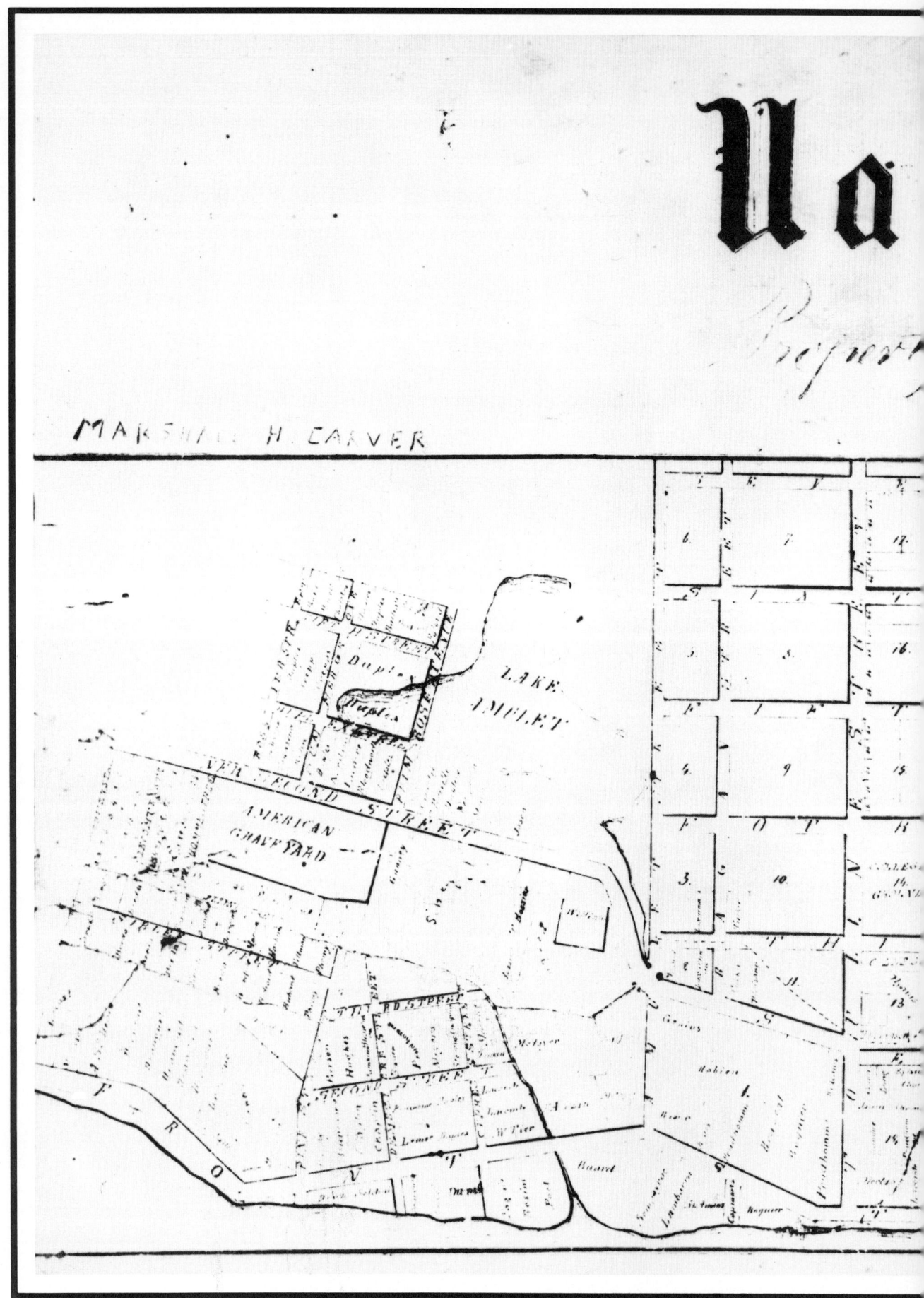

... The parish seat is Natchitoches which is an old town of French origin, and largely populated now by descendants of the original Creole settlers. The town has been in its decadence, from a business point of view, for many years, but in many respects it is a great place. Some of the finest specimens of architecture in the shape of churches, cathedrals and public buildings are to be seen here. It has always been noted for its social prestige and the wealth and polish of its citizens.

F. H. Tompkins, *North Louisiana*, 1886

Marshall H. Carver Collection, NSU Archives

Red River cotton steamers *New Era* and *Era No. 8*

Melrose Collection, NSU Archives

When the first steamboat to reach Natchitoches arrived in 1824 it found awaiting it a river trade already a century old. Trade needed no "working up." It merely shifted from dugout and flatboat to steamboat.

J. E. Guardia, "Historic Natchitoches, Louisiana: Its Two-Century Raison d'Etre," Melrose Collection, NSU Archives

1865 letter about shipping cotton from Ducournau landing

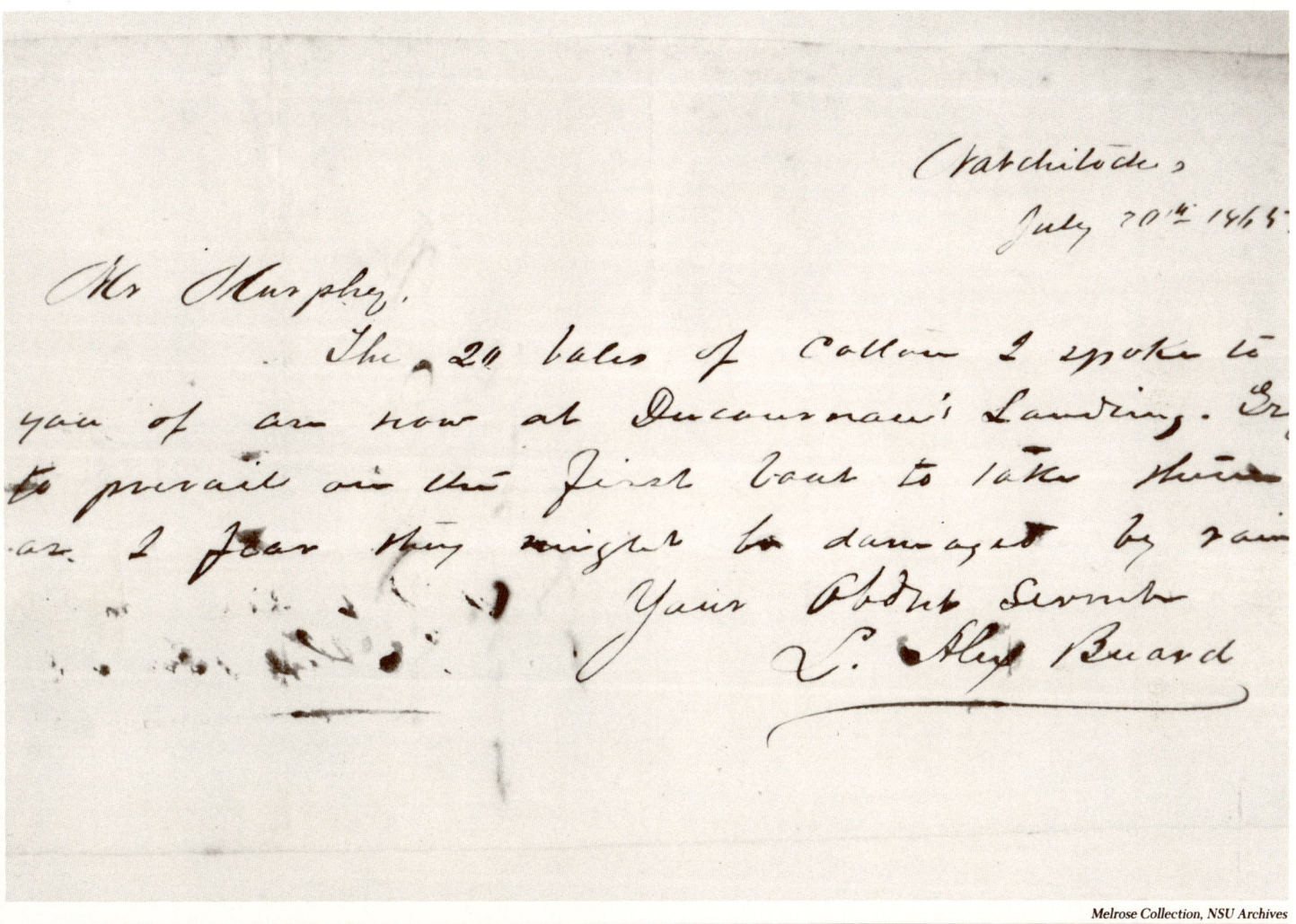

Melrose Collection, NSU Archives

The great fault which I find at this post is the river, which is very difficult during six months of the year, not having water for navigation ... but during high water, all the channels fill and can be navigated with boats — which is in the months from January to July. But it is necessary to have Indian guides because the French do not know all the channels, which are not all navigable.

Derbanne: *Report of the Post of Natchitoches, 1723* (translated by Katherine Bridges and Winston DeVille)

Natchitoches Parish Courthouse

Melrose Collection, NSU Archives

Do you remember the old town clock
That hung in the courthouse tower?
Day in and day out, year in and year out,
Striking each quarter hour.
                Grace Tarleton Aaron

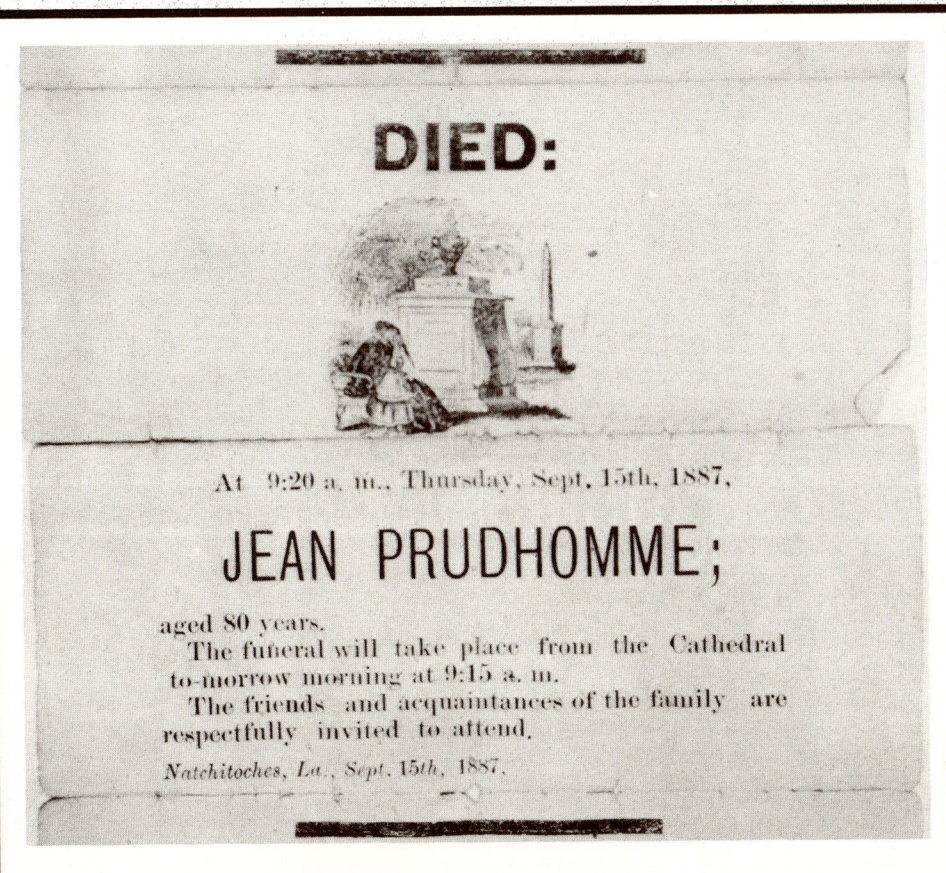

There seemed some sort of curious connection between the lives of these people and the soft white material with which their existence had been so closely interwoven — as though their very circumstances had partaken of the same quality. What it had done to them — this thing that was once the strength of the country and was now so powerless to bring prosperity.
  William Spratling, "Cane River Portraits"

Funeral notices

Melrose Collection, NSU Archives

Ox team crossing Cane River

Melrose Collection, NSU Archives

... when the Red River changed its main bed at the village of Grand Ecore, four miles north of Natchitoches, and carved out a new route that rejoined the old course far downstream, all of this was altered. Natchitoches, left orphaned on a measly trickle, was bereft of river commerce and Grand Ecore became for a time the metropolis of the river. It was not until the twentieth century that the anemic river to Natchitoches was dammed and converted into the lovely Cane River Lake.

James Aswell, "The Town the G.I.s Called 'Smith.'"

Cane River bridge looking toward East Natchitoches

Robert DeBlieux Collection, NSU Archives

Cane River winds its graceful way. It is a lake now. In the town of Natchitoches they say Cane River "was sired by God and damned by Phanor Breazeale."

                                          Meigs O. Frost

I struck Red River in August, 1865, nearly forty-three years ago ... The banks of Red River, from the mouth to Kiomatia, a distance of one thousand miles — were lined with cotton, and the only question asked by shippers of the Captain of the boat was: "How many bales will you take?" The freight on cotton from upper Red River at that time to New Orleans was $50.00 per bale. Boats on Red River were as thick as leaves in ambrosia.

    Captain M. L. Scovell

Steamer *Scovell* at Twenty-four-mile Landing, Cohen Plantation.
Frank Scovell, master
George Adams, clerk
John Clark, mate
Wm. Redman and T. M. Wells, pilots
Bob Bowman, engineer
Dave White and Ike Walcott, stewards

Photo given to Robert B. DeBlieux by Joseph Henry Sr., in Robert DeBlieux Collection, NSU Archives

Just at the edge of town on a high hill that overlooks the old churches, the tangled graveyards, the sweet rose gardens and the blue ribbon of rivers, there stands the normal school, a state institution of which we may all well be proud. It is a fine, mellow old mansion with deep porches and huge columns, a grand old building not unlike our city hall. It is old and shaky in some of the joints, but perhaps some day in an excess of virtue some legislature may give the money to repair and beautify it. It has now been in operation for about four years, and it is one of our ventures into advanced methods that has paid well so far.

Catharine Cole, c. 1889

Pledge signed by Cammie Garrett

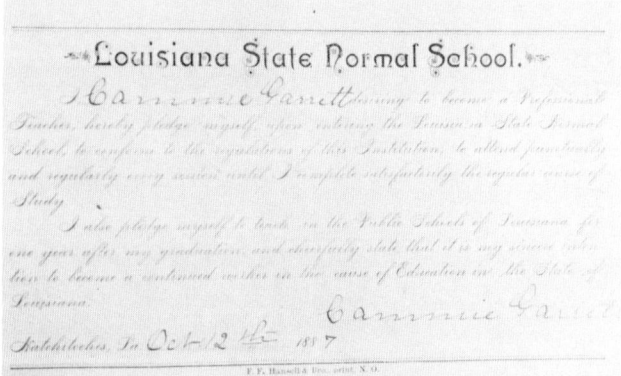

Melrose Collection, NSU Archives

I, Cammie Garrett, desiring to become a Professional Teacher, hereby pledge myself, upon entering the Louisiana State Normal School, to conform to the regulations of this Institution, to attend punctually and regularly every session until I complete satisfactorily the regular course of Study.

I also pledge myself to teach in the Public Schools of Louisiana for one year after my graduation, and cheerfully state that it is my sincere intention to become a continued worker in the cause of Education in the State of Louisiana.

Cammie Garrett
Natchitoches, La. Oct. 12th 1887

32 — CANE RIVER COUNTRY Louisiana

Louisiana State Normal School

Cammie Garrett [Henry]

George Williamson Collection, NSU Archives

Melrose Collection, NSU Archives

Sketch above by Willie Jack, 1889

George Williamson Collection, NSU Archives

George Williamson Collection, NSU Archives

Convent and Matron's Building, State Normal

CANE RIVER COUNTRY Louisiana — 33

Front Street at Touline, looking north

Melrose Collection, NSU Archives

New Inn Hotel, southwest corner of Front and Touline Streets

Melrose Collection, NSU Archives

Melrose Collection, NSU Archives

Front Street from across the river, 1927: (left to right) Mrs. Rogers millinery, New Inn Hotel, Elks Home, Motor Inn, Peoples Hardware, Peoples Furniture, J. & A. Prudhomme.

Service Station, Front Street south of the present Chamber of Commerce building.

Robert DeBlieux Collection, NSU Archives

Melrose Collection, NSU Archives

Front Street from across the river, 1927: (left to right) Ducournau, Kaffie General Mdse. & Hardware, Express Office, Gas Company, Natchitoches Motor Company, Frost & Johnson.

Natchitoches still cherishes her ancient ideals and traditions with a regard that borders on reverence, but in latter years has turned her face toward the future and is rapidly assuming her place in the very front rank of the progressive communities of the south. Of late old land marks have been swept away by the march of twentieth century progress. The hum of the hammer and saw is now heard on every hand and improvements that would fairly seem to stagger another city of like size are going on day by day until now the ancient aspect of the town to a degree is lost and a model city fashioned after the most progressive ideas of the twentieth century has reared its head.

Shreveport Times,
27 September 1903

First Bank of Natchitoches

Melrose Collection, NSU Archives

1892 telephone, Bermuda, La.

Courtesy Mrs. J. Alphonse Prudhomme

36 — CANE RIVER COUNTRY Louisiana

Julie C. Built by the Silsby Mfg. Co., Seneca Falls, N.Y. Cost $3,500.

This old fire-fighter was bought and delivered at Natchitoches in the Autumn of 1891. There was a big celebration upon the occasion, and it was christened "Julie C." in honor of Miss Julie Caspari, the most beautiful young lady of Natchitoches, and the daughter of Captain Caspari, one of its most enterprising citizens.

The ceremonies were conducted by Rev. Durier. At the time the engine was first tested it threw a stream of water from the lake on Front Street over the tower of the Methodist Church 100 ft. high and two blocks away.

When grading the site for the new depot, an old shed sheltering the discarded old engine and some other city equipment had to be removed, and it now stands near Trudeau Street unprotected and vandals have robbed it of its valves and even the name plate, like many things of its kind after outliving its usefulness it has no protector.

A. Babb, "My Sketch Book"

Melrose Collection, NSU Archives

Courtesy Mrs. J. Alphonse Prudhomme

Wooden oil derrick, "Blossom No. 1," Campti, 1913

Jefferson Street depot

Courtesy Mrs. J. Alphonse Prudhomme

"The common time necessary to make a voyage from Natchitoches to and from New Orleans is from thirty to forty days." So writes Mr. William Darby in his Geographical Description of Louisiana, Southern Mississippi and Alabama, published in 1817.

How things have changed! Now a single night's ride out of New Orleans in a palace car on the Texas and Pacific R.R., brings us to Cypress, twelve miles from Natchitoches. Here we change cars. The less said about breakfast the better! We never did believe in early breakfast anyway. The journey is finished on the Natchitoches Railroad.

Rev. Charles H. Crawford

Texas & Pacific train crew, c. 1905

Courtesy Mrs. J. Alphonse Prudhomme

38 — CANE RIVER COUNTRY Louisiana

Natchitoches Texas & Pacific Railroad station

Courtesy Mrs. J. Alphonse Prudhomme

Courtesy Mrs. J. Alphonse Prudhomme

Courtesy Mrs. J. Alphonse Prudhomme

Far left: Grand Ecore bridge.

Left: Bayou Natchez railroad station

The Natchitoches Railway and Construction company, an offspring of the Progressive League, is composed of the leading progressive citizens of the town of Natchitoches, who by voluntary subscriptions raised a fund in cash, which formed the nucleus of the capital with which the Grand Ecore bridge across the Red river was built. The tax payers of ward one, including the town of Natchitoches, voted a 5 mills tax and the police jury pledged a part of the regular revenues of the parish to meet the cost of the bridge, a modern steel structure erected at a cost of nearly $100,000. The bridge was completed and accepted in May, 1902, and since that time it has been open for the free use of the people, and has already proven a valuable feeder to the business interests of the town of Natchitoches, as well as a great convenience to the people.

Shreveport Times, 27 September 1903

After you are baptized, you must give up your sinful ways, and play and sing hymn-tunes, or spirituals, or 'ballots,' or 'jump-up' songs about folks in the Bible. Some of them are lively enough. There's that one beginning:

    Delilah wuz a woman,
    fine an' fair,
    Pleasant-lookin' wid her
    coal-black hair . . .

That was a grand one, with its surging refrain:

    Oh, if I wuz Sampson,
    I'd pull dat buildin' down!"
               Lyle Saxon, "Cane River"

Lyle Saxon photo, NSU Archives

Lyle Saxon photo, NSU Archives

Lyle Saxon photo, NSU Archives

Lyle Saxon photo, NSU Archives

CANE RIVER COUNTRY Louisiana — 41

Colfax ferry, confluence of the Cane and Red Rivers, 1921

Melrose Collection, NSU Archives

Natchitoches, the parish seat, has a population of 3,388. It is centrally located, is the most important trading and shipping point in the parish ... A small steamboat plies Cane River Lake. There is very little traffic on Red River.

The main country roads of the parish are good most of the year. Roads on the sandy front lands of the river bottoms are very good through winter and spring, but are somewhat heavy through the summer. Stretches in the stiff lands of the bottom are good in summer, but are at times impassable in winter.

U.S. Department of Agriculture, *Soil Survey of Natchitoches Parish, Louisiana, 1925*

The road to the Natchitoches depot, 1927

Melrose Collection, NSU Archives

The Texas and Pacific Railway has recently built a modern and beautiful passenger station in the City of Natchitoches. The people are justly proud of it and take pleasure in showing it to visitors. President Lancaster of the "TP" has the knack of putting beauty and dignity into structures built for useful purposes, without adding materially to the cost of them. The Natchitoches station is a notable example.

The main waiting room is a replica of the Master's Cabin of the Santa Maria, the famous little ship in which Columbus made his first voyage to the New World. Local color is given to it by making the drop from each chandelier, a reproduction of the hilt of the sword of St. Denis, the famous founder of Natchitoches.

W. R. Lence, "Historic Natchitoches," 1931

Right: Poster advertising a play by Hilda Perini
Below: Washington Street looking south

Melrose Collection, NSU Archives

Natchitoches ... is a very old town, having been established 100 years ago. There are many French and Spanish houses in it, and a considerable number of Spaniards still inhabit it ... and the opulent planters have houses in the town, for the sake of society. The people are excessively fond of balls and dancing. It has a respectable society, and a weekly newspaper, in French and English.

Timothy Flint, *A Condensed Geography and History of the Western States, or the Mississippi Valley*, 1828

Thomas Duckett Boyd, president of Louisiana State Normal, 1888-1896, with faculty and students

George Williamson Collection, NSU Archives

... The president, Col. Thomas D. Boyd, is the right man in the right place. The wonderful smoothness in the management of the school, the earnestness of the teachers, and the enthusiasm of the pupils, show what can be done by a man with a genius for administration, assisted by a corps of teachers who have a genuine interest in their life-work.
Official Journal of the Senate of the State of Louisiana, 1890

First crossing, Church Street bridge

The magnificent iron draw-bridge which spans Cane River opposite this city was built by the Youngstown Bridge Co., of Youngstown, Ohio. It was begun in September 1893, and finished in February, 1894. It is 16 feet wide, 480 feet long, and cost $15,500. This amount was raised, and the construction superintended, by the Natchitoches Cane River Bridge Co., a corporation which was organized for this purpose in 1890. The company raised by private subscription, $3500; the Parish contributed $6000 and the City of Natchitoches, $6000. The bridge is free and is owned jointly by the City and Parish of Natchitoches. Aside from its beauty and convenience to those who can now take pleasure drives along the beautiful banks of the Cane, without the expense and inconvenience of a ferry, it will add greatly to the large country business done by our merchants. The bridge is something we wanted, and needed badly. It is a lasting monument to the energy of its promoters, and a worthy testimonial to the enterprise of this community.

Commencement Bulletin issued by the Comus Club, Natchitoches, 26 May 1894

Giles W. Millspaugh, Jr., Collection, NSU Archives

Church Street bridge, looking east

Giles W. Millspaugh, Jr., Collection, NSU Archives

The Union Colonel Vifquin, quartered on the Tauzin family, suspected the Sacred Heart Convent as a possible storehouse for ammunition. After planting guns in the American Cemetery and training them on the school, he demanded that the institution submit to a thorough search. Mother Superior hoisted a white flag and gave the girls a few hasty words regarding good conduct. No sooner had the students caught sight of the Unionists than they shouted excitedly, "Yankees! Yankees! Come see the Yankees!" For this breach of etiquette the students were penalized for a week; a letter of formal apology was forwarded to Colonel Vifquin. Needless to say that the search proved fruitless in yielding either ammunition or fugitives.

    Sister Mary Silverius Karnowski, "Natchitoches During the Civil War and Reconstruction Period"

Federal troops quartered at Sacred Heart Academy (Bullard Mansion) c. 1876

George Williamson Collection, NSU Archives

> The house was a six-room, long, shambling affair, shrinking together from decrepitude. There was not an entire pane of glass in the structure; and the Turkey-red curtains flapped in and out of the broken apertures.
>
> Kate Chopin, *Bayou Folk*

Aubert Roque house at its original site

Robert DeBlieux Collection, NSU Archives

Aubert Roque house on the Cane Riverfront

Courtesy B. A. Cohen

Laying bricks on Front Street

Robert DeBlieux Collection, NSU Archives

Old Natchitoches Parish jail

Giles W. Millspaugh, Jr., Collection, NSU Archives

Renting a crystal clear stillness, deep-throated comes stealing
The great bell of the Immaculate Conception, — white robed angels are kneeling.
⊕ ⊕ ⊕
And when night's falling shadows e'er Natchitoches steal
Rings the Angelus; its benediction one's very soul feels.
                                    Mrs. L. V. Tarver, "The Angelus"

Church of the Immaculate Conception, 1898

Israel Suddath

There were those who declared Uncle Israel to be illiterate, and he never argued the point. He stoutly maintained, however, that in the years following slavery, he had a vision one night in which the Lord appeared. During this visitation Uncle Israel had promised the Almighty that if God would only let him have sufficient understanding to read the Bible, he would never read any other page in print. The Lord readily entered in to the agreement, as the story went, and it wasn't long before Uncle Israel had found himself a church, Primer (i.e. "Plymouth") Rock, across the river.

He always carried his Bible with him and his congregation, not fussy about the finer theological points, always seemed satisfied with the message flowing from his lips, once he had mounted the pulpit, opened the Good Book and begun his oration.

François Mignon,
Plantation Memo, 1972

Courtesy Joseph Henry, Sr.

Israel Suddath's loyalty oath, 1867

United States of America,
STATE OF LOUISIANA.

Original No. 9__ 11 Ward District.

REGISTER'S OFFICE,

PARISH OF Natchitoches

OATH.

"I, Isral Suddath do solemnly swear, or affirm, in the presence of Almighty God, that I am a citizen of the State of Louisianee, that I have resided in said State for Twelve months next preceding this day, and now reside in the county of _____ or the parish of Natchitoches in said State, as the case may be; that I am twenty-one years old; that I have not been disfranchised for participation in any rebellion or civil war against the United States, nor for felony committed against the laws of any of the United States; that I have never been a member of any State Legislature, nor held any executive or judicial office in any State, and afterwards engaged in insurrection or rebellion against the United States, and given aid or comfort to the enemies thereof; that I have never taken an oath as a member of Congress of the United States, or as an officer of the United States, or as a member of any State Legislature, or as an executive or judicial officer of any State, to support the Constitution of the United States, and afterwards engaged in insurrection and rebellion against the United States, or given aid or comfort to the enemies thereof: that I will faithfully support the Constitution and obey the laws of the United States, and will, to the best of my ability, encourage others so to do. So help me God."

Isral his
        X   Suddath
       mark

I do hereby certify that on this 25th day of May 1867 appeared before me Isral Suddath who subscribed to the foregoing oath.

C Ferguson
Register.

DUPLICATE.

Melrose Collection, NSU Archives

Mule team used in building railroad

Giles W. Millspaugh, Jr., Collection, NSU Archives

September 9, 1852. The Police Jury of this parish in session today promised $250,000 payable in 5 successive yearly installments to be levied by tax on the real estate of this parish, the whole to be employed in the making of a railroad from this place connecting with the New Orleans and Opelousas railroad. This ordinance shall not be binding until approved by a majority of the legal voters of the parish. The election on this question will take place on the first Tuesday of November, the day immediately following the presidential election.

October 8, Friday. Mr. P. G. Campbell left for Cloutierville, where he has been invited to make a speech, at a Railroad Barbecue to be held there tomorrow.

October 10, Sunday. We got news of the Cloutierville Railroad Barbecue. The whole thing went off admirably, and there was some fine speaking done, by I. G. Campbell, Hyams and Henry Hertzog on the railroad movement. The latter spoke in French.

November 3, Wednesday . . . The vote went here in favor of the Democrats and rail road tax.

[typed copy] Lestan Prudhomme Diary, Melrose Collection

Railroad cut at Chopin

Giles W. Millspaugh, Jr., Collection, NSU Archives

Of recent years, the Natchitoches railroad has been built to Cypress, some twelve miles distant on the Texas and Pacific railroad, through which the town has regular communication with all trains on that great road. Captain L. Caspari, the President of the Natchitoches railroad is one of the leading and most enterprising residents of the town and not only is he to be credited for the construction of this road, but for the establishment of the State Normal School, at Natchitoches, for which he worked like a beaver while representing his parish in the Legislature ... The Natchitoches railroad is being extended in the direction of Shreveport; an iron bridge is about to be constructed, both of which will greatly increase the business of the town.

Louisiana Review, 1893

Ceremony of turning on the first gas in Natchitoches, at a building on St. Denis Street, c. 1926

Giles W. Millspaugh, Jr., Collection, NSU Archives

Washington Street, 1907

Marcia Harrison Collection, NSU Archives

Marcia Harrison Collection, NSU Archives

Normal Campus, 1907

What I recommended to our committee and what it in turn recommended to the State Board relative to the home economics cottage is that we should erect, instead of a $16,000 or $18,000 two-story fireproof building such as we had under consideration six months ago, a modest cottage of frame construction such as our girls are likely to use when they go out into the world and perhaps take charge of homes. The head of our department of home economics, Miss Weeks, who is now away on leave of absence, never approved the plan of spending a large sum of money on her cottage. Lately she had been very strong in the conviction that the cottage should not cost over $5,000 or $6,000. To be on the safe side, our committee recommended that we set aside $7,000. My plan is to have an ordinary sketch made by one of our local builders: buy the material ourselves: and have the building erected under the direct supervision of our superintendent. In other words, the house would be built in the same way in which a number of people here in Natchitoches have erected houses in the last two or three years.

In fact I have had a rough sketch made already, and it appears that we shall be able to erect the necessary cottage with four bedrooms, living room, dining room, kitchen, two bath rooms, a large sleeping porch, and closets in every bedroom, for something less than $6,000.

    Letter from President V. L.
    Roy to Hon. J. N. Gourdain,
    19 September 1924

CANE RIVER COUNTRY Louisiana — 57

U. S. Monitor *Osage* on Red River

U. S. Navy photograph

Report of Colonel Brent, Confederate States Army, regarding engagement with Federal fleet near junction of Cane and Red Rivers, April 26-27, 1864.

✧✧✧

On the morning of the 26th of April two gunboats of the enemy, one an iron-plated monitor, supposed to be the *Osage*, and the other of the class called tin-clad, mounting eight guns and protected by about an inch of iron, were discovered lying near DeLoach's Bluff, in Red River.

Benton's rifle section, Captain Benton commanding, and Nettle's smoothbore section, Lieutenant Smith commanding (Captain Nettles present), supported by Major Williams with a battalion of sharp-shooters, were placed in position and opened fire on the tin-clad who, after severe punishment, rapidly fled after an engagement of thirty minutes.

The iron-plated monitor poured a heavy enfilading fire on the artillery and its support, but no attention was paid to it, in obedience to general artillery orders not to reply to the fire of the iron-plated monitors, and our whole fire was directed on the eight-gun gunboat.

Grand Ecore ferry

Robert DeBlieux Collection, NSU Archives

It's the Cane, Cane, Cane River
Country . . .
Ex-home of ole steam boats
That used to ply the river bed
With cattle, pigs and goats . . .
The age-old town of Natchi-
toches . . .
Grillwork, bricks made by hand
Lives on despite time's
changing trends . . .
In the Cane River Country Land.

Norm Fletcher, *The Cane
River Country Land,* © 1976

The *W. T. Scovell* at Front Street, 1908

Robert DeBlieux and Giles W. Millspaugh, Jr., Collections, NSU Archives

CANE RIVER COUNTRY Louisiana — 59

How do you like to walk out on the street,
Outside the stile, so free?
Oh, I do think it the jolliest feat
Ever the people see.

Over the bridge, and 'round and 'round,
Led by a teacher tall,
Till boys and houses and towns seem bound
By teacher, pupils and all.

Down one walk, up another side,
Back to the corner, then
Around the first walk we laughing stride,
And up the other again.

While people look down on our countless throng,
Down on the merry file,
Till up the street we go marching along,
Back to the Normal stile.

Potpourri, 1911

Robert DeBlieux Collection, NSU Archives

Giles W. Millspaugh, Jr., Collection, NSU Archives

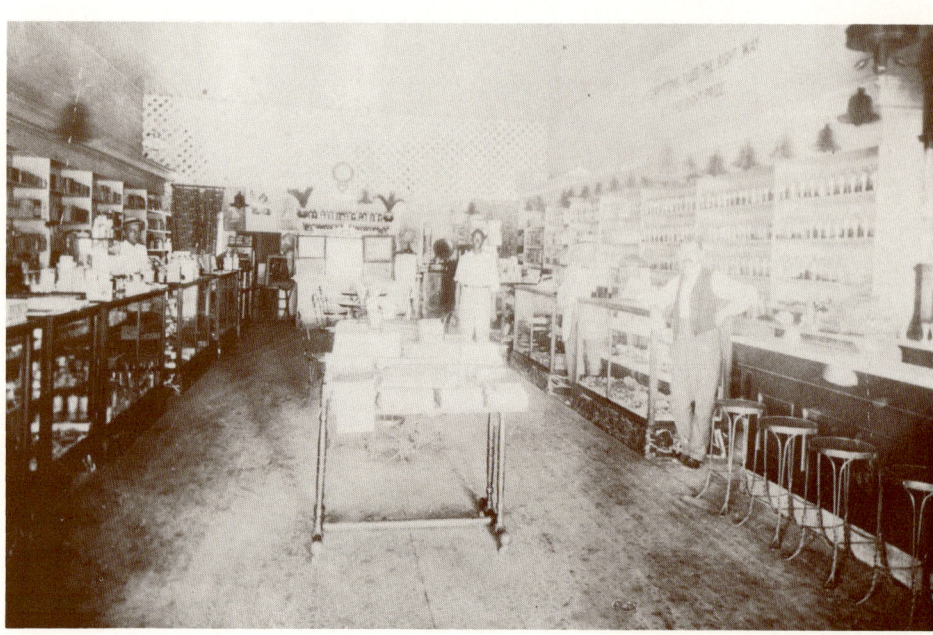

Giles W. Millspaugh, Jr., Collection, NSU Archives

Top: Natchitoches from the east side of Cane River
Center: McClung's Drug Store
Right: McClung's Drug Store

Two views of Front Street on Trades Day

Robert DeBlieux Collection, NSU Archives

Robert DeBlieux Collection, NSU Archives

CANE RIVER COUNTRY Louisiana — 61

The well organized practice school, the new manual training rooms, the laboratories and library, the ventilating system in the academic building, the baths and screens in the dormitories, the beautiful grounds, with forest, lake and swimming pool, guarantee a delightful experience to those who come to take advantage of the excellent courses offered.
Louisiana State Normal School Catalog, 1911-1912

There's a perfectly, handsomely, youngiful boy
Outside the stile just a-talking,
And the beautiful, uglyful, wishiful girls
Want to and can't go a-walking.
Potpourri, 1912

George Williamson Collection, NSU Archives

Three views of the entrance to the Louisiana State Normal School

George Williamson Collection, NSU Archives

George Williamson Collection, NSU Archives

62 — CANE RIVER COUNTRY Louisiana

Normal Hill, from the lake

> Oh! Who will walk a while with me along
>   this oft-trod way?
> A path where comrades of old times and
>   new
> From one another deepest secrets drew
> Or lingered, as each sunny space was
>   passed,
> To watch the silent shadow-patterns cast.
> *Potpourri*, 1912

George Williamson Collection, NSU Archives

Old Normal Walk with the convent building in the background

George Williamson Collection, NSU Archives

CANE RIVER COUNTRY Louisiana — 63

Hear the mellow dinner Bells,
   Iron Bells!
What a world of rice and beans
   their harmony foretells,
Through the balmy evening night
Or the happy noontime bright,
From the molten iron notes
   From all around,
What a feeling floats
To the hungry girl that listens,
   while she gloats
     On the sound.
       Potpourri, 1909

George Williamson Collection, NSU Archives

George Williamson Collection, NSU Archives

Views of the Louisiana State Normal School.
Top: library interior.
Center: tennis courts.
Bottom: dining hall.

George Williamson Collection, NSU Archives

64 — CANE RIVER COUNTRY Louisiana

Giles W. Millspaugh, Jr., Collection, NSU Archives

Between the twilight and bedtime,
When the night is beginning to fall,
Comes a pause in the girls' conversation
That is known as the Study Hall.

We hear in the chambers above us
The sound of Mrs. Keane's feet;
The noise of a door that is opening,
And a voice saying, soft and sweet:

"Girls, don't you know you must study?
We must not have any play,
Or tomorrow I'll have to report you,
And what will the President say?"
    Potpourri, 1911

Giles W. Millspaugh, Jr., Collection, NSU Archives

Giles W. Millspaugh, Jr., Collection, NSU Archives

Views of the Louisiana State Normal School.
Top: Matron's Building
Center: Convent Building
Bottom: The Quadrangle

By and by we came to an extensive meadow, interspersed with small plantations of tobacco and Indian corn; and here I could perceive on an eminence before us a square space, inclosed with large palisadoes standing close to each other, and driven into the ground. This I learned served as a fort to the settlement; beyond which, and at some distance, stood a number of little wooden houses, in a straight line but at large intervals from one another. They might amount, with a few others, which appeared scattered over the country, to the number of seventy, and constituted the whole French settlement on this part of Red River. The village and fort command an extensive prospect on the opposite side of the river; a prospect presenting a large meadow bounded on all sides by the woods, and plentifully stocked with cows and horses.

I lived here with the proprietor of the canoe, but was miserably accommodated, both in diet and lodging. The house was small, and dirty in the extreme; and our bread, made of rice mixed with Indian corn, was of the very worst quality ... It is difficult for the reader to imagine how much the air on Red River is contaminated by the horrid stench which arises from the urine and excrements of the alligator. Our biscuit was so impregnated with this horrible effluvia, that it had acquired the nauseous taste of rotten musk, but I supported my spirits under all those hardships with the prospect of making a short stay in this country.

The settlement of Natchitoches is computed to be a hundred and forty leagues NW from New Orleans; is of small extent, but tolerably populous; and the inhabitants, like all those of Louisiana are lively, well-formed in their persons, and inured to fatigue.

Pierre Marie Francois, Vicomte de Pages, *Travels Round the World in the Years 1768, 1769, 1770, 1771.* London, 1791-92

View of Natchitoches

Saint Augustine Church, Isle Brevelle

Melrose Collection, NSU Archives

Marcotte's map, NSU Archives

CANE RIVER COUNTRY Louisiana— 67

Mrs. Cammie G. Henry

Courtesy Joseph Henry, Sr.

The cabin is a home-made studio; its furnishings are carefully planned to be in keeping. This bed, the mattress, is handmade, too. Made on Melrose plantation. I saw them drying the moss with which it is stuffed, behind the plantation store. Saw the old negro woman, "pickin' " it free of sticks and leaves. That is the stuffing of the studio mattress. Its artistic cover, needless to say, was made by Mrs. Henry herself.

Mary Belle McKellar, "Melrose"

A cotton quilt made at Melrose

Melrose Collection, NSU Archives

It's the Cane, Cane, Cane River Country . . .
So rich in cotton white . . .
Where man does work so all the day . . .
And lays to rest at night . . .
The bullfrogs bark a lusty song . . .
And crickets chirp in bands . . .
While moonbeams paint the lily pads . . .
In the Cane River Country Land.
The Cane River Country Land
© 1976, Norm Fletcher

CANE RIVER COUNTRY Louisiana — 69

When I remember roadsides as they used to be, then look at the glaring speedways of today, I ask myself, after all, is *speed* the most important thing in the world? We drove to the country to see the dogwood in spring, the glory of maple and sweetgum in fall.
   Caroline Dormon,
   Natives Preferred

Robert DeBlieux Collection, NSU Archives

Robert DeBlieux Collection, NSU Archives

Robert DeBlieux Collection, NSU Archives

Three views of the opening of the Jefferson Highway (Highway 6)

Little by little the Joyous Coast was changing. The old rutted dirt road that fringed the Cane had been abandoned. The highway cut through the swamps and marshy lands and fields full of corn and refused to follow the shim of the river... It even plowed its way through people's dooryards, rooting up ancient landmarks: oaks and chinas and gnarled crepe-myrtles, their branches bowed to the earth with bloom...

Ada Jack Carver,
"Singing-Woman"

Left: Mrs. Etta Levy and the first airplane in town
Below: Occupants of the car are not identified

Robert DeBlieux Collection, NSU Archives

Courtesy Mrs. J. Alphonse Prudhomme

CANE RIVER COUNTRY Louisiana — 71

Old St. Mary's Academy buildings

Melrose Collection, NSU Archives

St. Mary's Academy occupies a high rank. Situated near the center of the town, for beauty and healthfulness, the site cannot be excelled. Its commodious buildings stand upon a hill overlooking the Cane river valley ... The house is a three story building, with separate departments for boys and girls. The building is furnished with all the modern contrivances which insure the health and comfort of teachers and pupils.

The male and female departments are separated entirely, but are similarly arranged. On the lower floor is found a well stocked library containing dictionaries, encyclopedias, histories and other works designed to assist the students ...

The house dates its origin back to 1846 when it was occupied by the ladies of the Sacred Heart. After their removal to a larger and more comfortable convent in 1856, the buildings were used for St. Joseph College, established under the auspices of Bishop Martin.

The College was subsequently removed and the house again occupied as a convent by the Sisters of Mercy (about the year 1870). After some seven or eight years of labor they also left, from which time until 1888 no other religious institution was established.

In September of the above mentioned year, five sisters of Divine Providence arrived at Natchitoches from San Antonio, Texas, for the purpose of opening a boarding and day school. Their coming was at the request of Bishop Durier, of the diocese.

Commencement Bulletin issued by the Comus Club, 26 May 1894

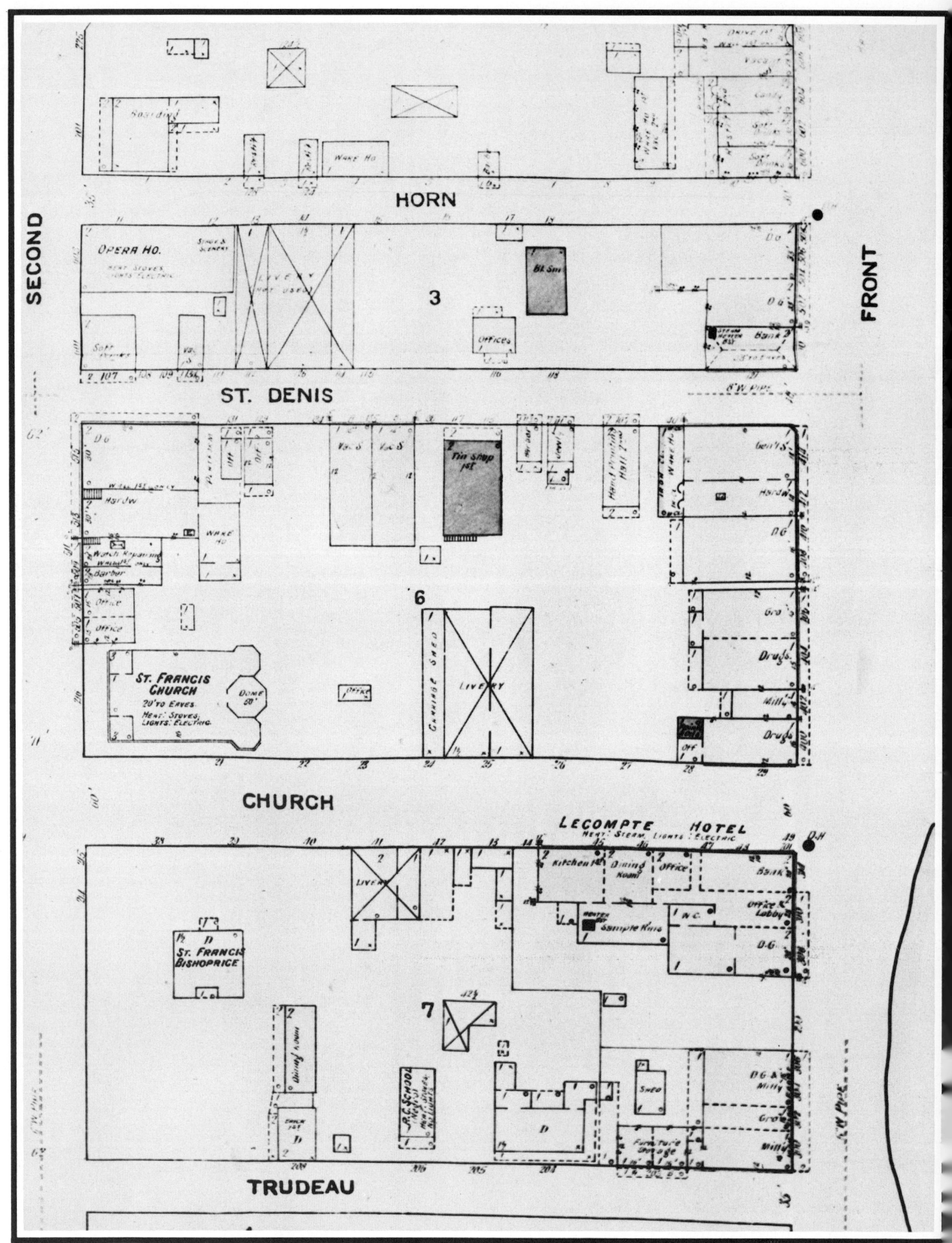

Portion of the Sanborn Map of Natchitoches, May 1909

74 — CANE RIVER COUNTRY Louisiana

Courtesy Tommy G. Johnson

Highway 1 North

Rail fence in Natchitoches Parish

Courtesy Tommy G. Johnson

Cattle graze on ranch at Cloutierville

Courtesy Tommy G. Johnson

CANE RIVER COUNTRY Louisiana — 75

Courtesy Robert DeBlieux

Courtesy Tommy G. Johnson

Courtesy B. A. Cohen

**Top: wooden cotton press at Magnolia Plantation.
Above left: cotton picker.
Above right: cotton on gin platform.**

Courtesy Tommy G. Johnson

Courtesy Tommy G. Johnson

Courtesy Tommy G. Johnson

**Top: Magnolia Plantation store.
Above: magnolia blossom.
Left: Old gasoline pump, Melrose.**

CANE RIVER COUNTRY Louisiana — 77

Right: Old River.
Below: Saline Lake.

Courtesy Tommy G. Johnson

Courtesy Tommy G. Johnson

Courtesy Tommy G. Johnson

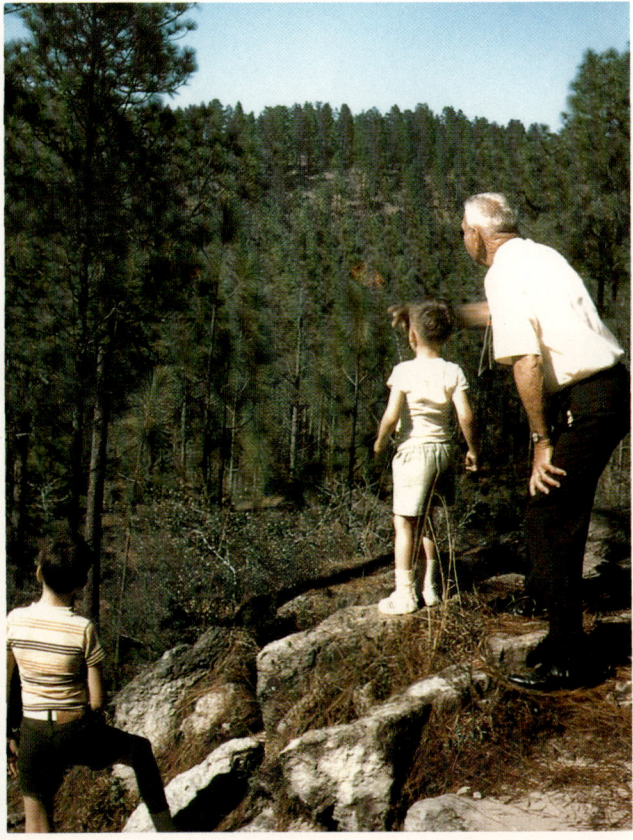

Left: Kisatchie Forest.
Below: Trees in watercolor by Mary Belle DeVargas.
Bottom: Saline Lake.

Courtesy NSU Archives

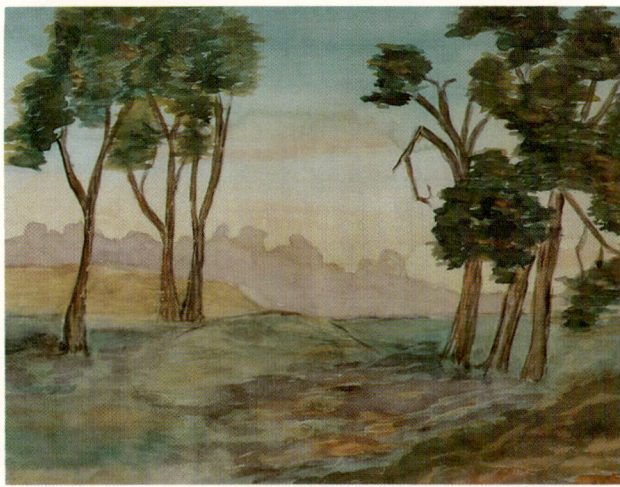

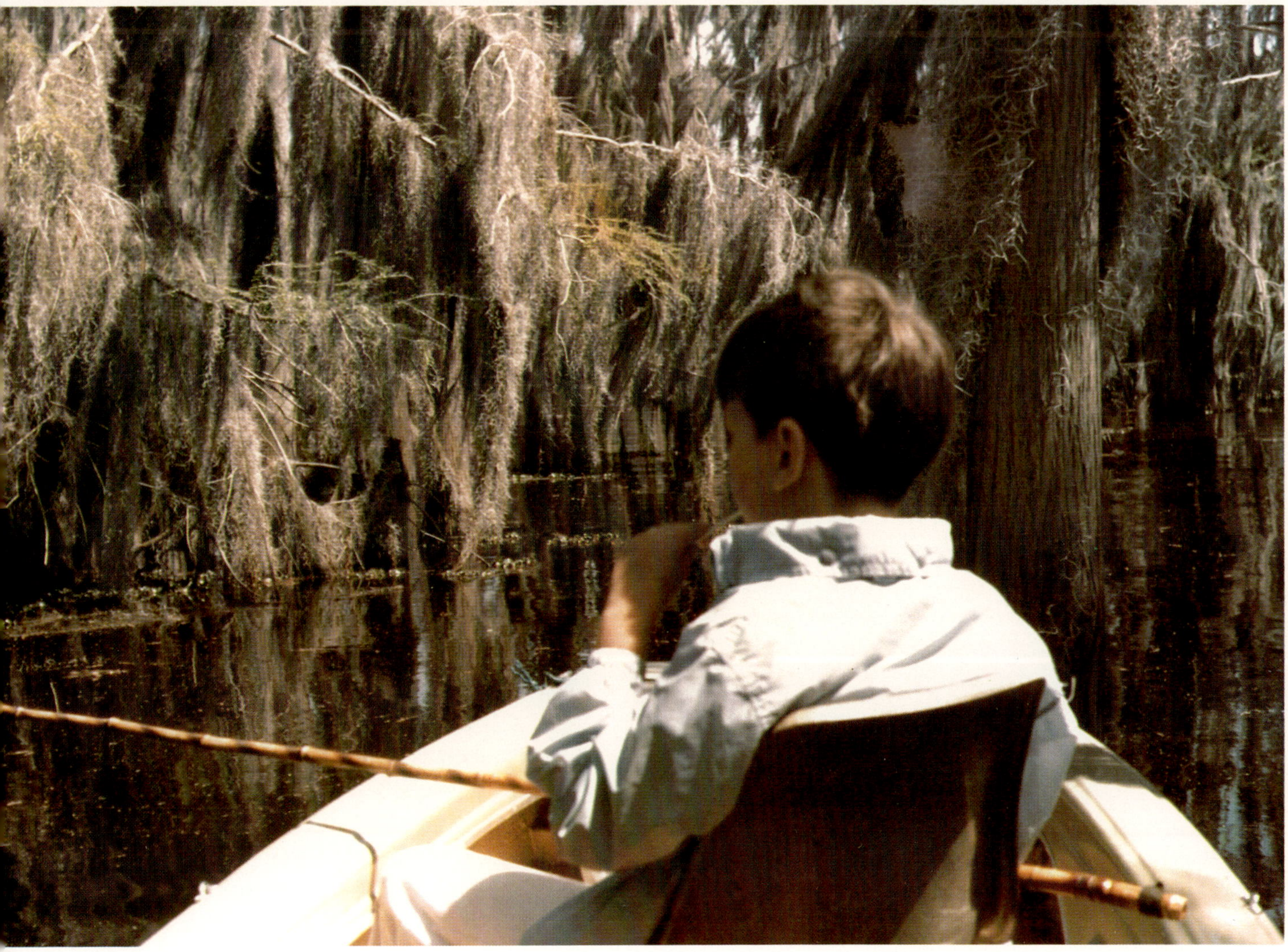

Courtesy Tommy G. Johnson

Prudhomme-Rouquier House, now owned by The Service League of Natchitoches, Inc.

Courtesy B. A. Cohen

Waterfall in Kisatchie National Forest

Courtesy Mrs. John Kyser; photo by the late Dr. John Kyser

CANE RIVER COUNTRY Louisiana — 81

Right: Cane River cabin scene.
Below: bridge near Sang Pour Sang.

Courtesy Mrs. Mina McKaskle

Courtesy Mary Carolyn Roberts

Beau Fort Plantation

Courtesy the Service League of Natchitoches, Inc., ©Cane River Cuisine; photo by John C. Guillet

Right: Old Russell Cemetery fence, gate.
Below: Mansfield Confederate Park

Courtesy Mary Carolyn Roberts

Courtesy Tommy G. Johnson

84 — CANE RIVER COUNTRY Louisiana

Left: Fort Jesup.
Below: Rebel State Park, Marthaville.

Courtesy B. A. Cohen

Courtesy B. A. Cohen

CANE RIVER COUNTRY Louisiana — 85

Below: J. H. Williams home. Bottom: Larry Taylor home.

Courtesy Tommy G. Johnson

Courtesy B. A. Cohen

Left: Ironwork silhouetted by a sunset.
Below: Old Natchitoches train station.

Courtesy Don Sepulvado

Courtesy Mary Carolyn Roberts

CANE RIVER COUNTRY Louisiana — 87

Clementine Hunter abstract.

Courtesy Mrs. Carol Wells

"Picking cotton", a primitive by Clementine Hunter.

Courtesy NSU Archives

Courtesy B. A. Cohen

Courtesy B. A. Cohen

Courtesy B. A. Cohen

Left: a trilogy of Bermuda (water pump), Melrose (spinning wheel), and Natchez (water well, bucket). **Below:** George Lewis home, Isle Brevelle.

Courtesy Adrian's Photography

Courtesy Tommy G. Johnson

Above: Sunset silhouettes church on Magnolia Plantation.
Right: a robin poses

Courtesy Harold Wales

90 — CANE RIVER COUNTRY Louisiana

... magnolia leaves gleamed and seemed to smile in the sunshine. Hardy rosevines clinging to old stuccoed pillars plumed themselves and bristled their leaves with satisfaction. And the violets peeped out to see if it was all over.

"Ah! this is a southern day," I uttered with deep gratification as I leisurely crossed the bridge afoot. A warm, gentle breeze was stirring. On the opposite side, a dear old lady was standing in her dear old doorway for me.

    Kate Chopin, "A December Day in Dixie"

Plank walk across Cane River, 1914

Giles W. Millspaugh, Jr., Collection, NSU Archives

View of Natchitoches from the East bank, turn of the century

Giles W. Millspaugh, Jr., Collection, NSU Archives

Below: Natchitoches Brass Band, 1905
Bottom: Louisiana State Normal baseball team, 1903/4

In the ball team picture are George Williamson, with hat in center; players Marcus Dismukes, Frank Cook, Sidney Cook, [---] Raggio, [---] Raggio; others not identified.

Giles W. Millspaugh, Jr., Collection, NSU Archives

Giles W. Millspaugh, Jr., Collection, NSU Archives

A well-lighted and ventilated room, occupying the main portion of the second story of Boyd Hall and formerly used as an auditorium, is now used as a gymnasium... Most of the athletic work required of students is done outdoors. This consists chiefly of basket-ball, tennis, volley ball, football, baseball and track work, for each of which the necessary courts are provided.
Louisiana State Normal College Catalog, 1921.

Giles W. Millspaugh, Jr., Collection, NSU Archives

**Left: Gymnastics class, Spring 1921.
Below: Natchitoches baseball team.**

Giles W. Millspaugh, Jr., Collection, NSU Archives

The plantation was very quiet, with that stillness which broods over broad, clean acres that furnish no refuge for so much as a bird that sings. The negroes were scattered about the fields at work, with hoe and plow, under the sun . . .

Kate Chopin, *Bayou Folk.*

Melrose Collection, NSU Archives

Melrose Collection, NSU Archives

The road into the town drops out of the purple mist of the hillsides and follows the winding thread of Cane River, past neglected, weed-choked fields, past singing willows, moist and cool, past a ravine overhung with tropic verdure, past outlying negro cabins bright with gaudy sunflowers, past a sunlit waste of bitter-weed, — and, its momentum spent with the long descent, straggles by the picket fence of the old Lamarie home.
Ada Jack Carver, "The Joyous Coast."

Left: Natchitoches Art Colony paintings on display.
Below: Natchitoches Art Colony cabin.

Melrose Collection, NSU Archives

Melrose Collection, NSU Archives

It is lazy and sweet along the Côte Joyeuse and on into the piney red-clay hills; for Time has been kind to Natchitoches. At the Resurrection season every year an Art Colony descends upon it with pallet and brush to paint its decaying witchery against the glory of massed crepe-myrtles.
Ada Jack Carver, "Redbone."

CANE RIVER COUNTRY Louisiana — 95

Right: Palace Cafe, Front Street
Below: Live Oak Hotel, Second and St. Denis Streets, burned c. 1933.

Melrose Collection, NSU Archives

Melrose Collection, NSU Archives

Left: Live Oak Corner, 1911
Below: Live Oak Corner

Robert DeBlieux Collection, NSU Archives

Melrose Collection, NSU Archives

I feel that, as things are here, & are likely to remain, I ought to hunt a new home; for my own & the children's sake.... It is true that we are cursed beyond measure by misgovernment, & that, owing to my intense disgust at the corruptions about me, & my uncomplying, (bad perhaps) temper, I have not, since the war, made a living at my profession, & that we have even suffered from want of clothing, every one of us, & been otherwise destitute, in consequence; & that now, things have arrived to that point that even the most compliant, the most cringingly & corrupt, supple, can glean but scarcity in the impoverished field. Yet I am loth to give up.
Henry Safford
Safford Collection, NSU Archives

My favorite walk is down a hill, along a winding path, between my house and the pond. It twists and dips and rises, with an occasional shrub, and around that a new vista. Where there is a sudden small drop, one or two flat brown rocks have been sunk to serve as steps. Here native azaleas have done well . . .
— Caroline Dormon, *Natives Preferred*

Right: De Soto Commission appointment signed by President Franklin D. Roosevelt.
Below: Caroline Dormon at Briarwood.

Below: Caroline Dormon at "Grandpappy" tree.
Lower left: "Wild Cherry", a seedling of two Abbeville irises, drawn by Caroline Dormon.
Lower right: "Southern reed-cane", drawn by Caroline Dormon.

Caroline Dormon Collection, NSU Archives

September 4, 1964
. . . the committee unanimously recommends the nomination of Miss Dormon for the honorary degree of Doctor of Science. The bases for such a nomination are:
1. Her publications as a botanist and botanical illustrator.
2. Her services to forestry conservation, in particular her promotion of Kisatchie National Forest.
3. Her contributions to horticulture through publications, lectures, and successful experiments in hybridizing Louisiana irises.
4. Her services to archeological and ethnological studies of the American Indian, especially as a member of the DeSoto Expedition Commission.

  Cecil G. Taylor, Dean, College of Arts and Sciences, Louisiana State University.

Caroline Dormon Collection, NSU Archives

Caroline Dormon Collection, NSU Archives

CANE RIVER COUNTRY Louisiana — 99

Wednesday March 30   The road all the way to Natchitoches, a distance of 18 miles one could say was a solid flame, and the air was completely permeated with the smell of burning cotton. My heart was filled with sadness at the sight of those lovely plantations in flames, and to see the work of the honest industry and perseverance of those good old Creole planters destroyed in the twinkling of an eye ... Tonight the enemy is camped 15 miles from Natchitoches. Thursday March 31   This morning, Natchitoches was completely evacuated by our authorities and I set out for Pleasant Hill ... and traveled through interminable pine forests ... This evening the enemy entered Natchitoches at 5 o'clock after a serious skirmish with our cavalry — two or three of our men were killed.

Felix Pierre Poché, *A Louisiana Confederate*

Courtesy B. A. Cohen

Courtesy B. A. Cohen

100 — CANE RIVER COUNTRY Louisiana

Ducournau Square area, now and then

Courtesy B. A. Cohen

Melrose Collection, NSU Archives

Methodist Church built early in the twentieth century and razed about 1954

Melrose Collection, NSU Archives

View of Natchitoches, July 1911

Melrose Collection, NSU Archives

> Over the roof of my neighbor's house
> An old magnolia tree
> Is appliqued upon the sky
> In leafy greenery.
> Grace Tarleton Aaron, "Magnolias"

Melrose Collection, NSU Archives

Melrose Collection, NSU Archives

It was the month of April . . . and the hot sun that had flamed since early dawn with a heat known only to southern lowlands, was at last casting long lazy shadows across the cabin with its rickety gallery and honeysuckle vine. No cloud appeared in the hot brassy sky with a promise of relief from the unusual heat that billowed in suffocating waves from the swamp and nearby canebrakes of the sluggish Bayou Pierre.

    Aida Mumford Gilvin and James Everett Mumford, *The Witch of Bayou Pierre*, 1939.

Melrose Collection, NSU Archives

Above: Breazeale Springs
Top left: crawfishing
Top right: boxing poster

CANE RIVER COUNTRY Louisiana — 103

Natchitoches Grammar School, Session of 1898-1899

George Williamson Collection, NSU Archives

The Natchitoches Grammar School

The old schoolhouse, which has lately been renovated, has seen three generations pass through its class-rooms, and is one of the old landmarks of the place. The school has been known by different names, and was, at times, but indifferently attended, until the opening of the Normal School gave an impetus to education.

Since then, some of its higher classes have been graded to facilitate the entrance of its pupils to the State Normal School as soon as they become of proper age.

It is now under the skillful management of Prof. Leon Greneaux and Miss M. Greneaux, who have raised it to its present standard. The former is a graduate of St. Louis University, Mo., and the latter of St. Michael's Convent, La., and also of the Lousiana State Normal School.

The number of pupils enrolled last session was 84, and several were refused admission for want of room.

It is now in a most prosperous condition, with the best of feeling existing between teachers, children and parents, which gives assurance of success.

26 May 1894, *Commencement Bulletin* published by the Natchitoches Comus Club

The Murphy family at Cherokee Plantation. Row one: Lou May Murphy, Linnie Murphy; seated behind: Robert Calvert Murphy, holding Emerson Murphy; Lee Tatum, George Robert Murphy, Martha Gully Murphy, Elizabeth Murphy Tatum, holding Perry Tatum. Standing: John Murphy, Fanny Murphy Hunsicker, Mattie Murphy.

Courtesy Mrs. William Nolan

Normal men, Fall, 1899 (1902-3 incorrect date)

Giles W. Millspaugh, Jr., Collection, NSU Archives

                State Normal School
                September 14, 1915

Men's Club Rules
We, the men of the Boy's Club, promise to enforce these regulations:
Article I
All rooms shall be inspected by monitors every morning . . .
Article II
In using the stools every one must be seated, or both boards must be turned back . . .
Article III
Rubbish must not be thrown in the slop jars or bath tubs or sinks . . .
Article IV
There shall be no smoking in the building at any time . . .
Article V
Everyone must be in bed and lights out at 10 o'clock . . .

President V. L. Roy and Normal College faculty, 1927

Giles W. Millspaugh, Jr., Collection, NSU Archives

Normal College Song
by Ross Maggio

Awake and praise our Alma Mater,
And let our hearts unfold;
Let us sing of brave vic-tries,
Of her traditions old.
Then let us stand and swear allegiance
And raise our banners high,
For Alma Mater ever honor
While from our hearts we cry
   Chorus
All hail Alma Mater;
All hail to our college,
The mother of wisdom,
The fountain of light;
And we make our pledges
To ever honor thee.
May God in his goodness
Protect her with His might.

... then for five long miles we passed on through a country the scenery of which would have made the heart of an artist leap with joy, and if could be reproduced on canvass would make the painter's fame and fortune, first along the banks of a spring stream, then across its silvery waters, then up the hillside to the crests where the rarified air as blew through the tall pines and green oaks would put the Colorado climate to shame, on and on we followed our leader, (Morris) Aaron, who was some time in the road and again would take a short cut with true woodsman's instinct where neither road nor bridal path marked the way, to the 'cut' where the foreign speculator had come and bought for a song the rich timber as far as the eye can reach, made a fortune and departed, leaving but a barren waste of stumps to remind us of our folly.
"Log of Hunting Party." 1905

Caroline Dormon Collection, NSU Archives

Courtesy Mrs. J. Alphonse Prudhomme

... Have you ever traveled through a real forest of long-leaf pines? Your syndicate owns a great area in the sand-hills of North Louisiana; as lovely a stretch of country as one can find. If you have ever seen it, I feel sure the beauty of it must have gripped you. There are large areas of this wild hill country where your tram lines have not yet penetrated. The clear streams are full of fish, the woods of birds and game; there are even a few deer and wild turkey still be be found there. The pines have not yet been gashed and marred by turpentining.

As you of course know, the longleaf pines are rapidly disappearing. Under existing conditions, they do not reforest; and, as things stand, in a short time they will be a memory..."

Caroline Dormon, 1920. Dormon Collection, NSU Archives

Top: Montrose logging camp, 1890. Dave Bains in the center
Below: Steam engines owned by the Weaver Brothers, Natchitoches Parish, early 20th century

Giles W. Millspaugh, Jr., Collection, NSU Archives

Giles W. Millspaugh, Jr., Collection, NSU Archives

Courtesy Mrs. J. Alphonse Prudhomme

Both photos: Oakland Plantation, Museum

Courtesy Mrs. J. Alphonse Prudhomme

110 — CANE RIVER COUNTRY Louisiana

Without the modern instruments for well-drilling, (P. Phanor) Prudhomme set about having his own made. To this task he assigned Solomon Williams, the plantation blacksmith... The augurs were exceptionally fine pieces of blacksmithing. They resembled machine-made tools more than the handiwork of a slave blacksmith. One of the augurs has a double point and is almost perfect in workmanship...
  W. S. Langier in *Times Picayune*, 4 March 1928

Left: Oakland Plantation museum.
Below: Oakland Plantation, slave-made well-drilling tools.

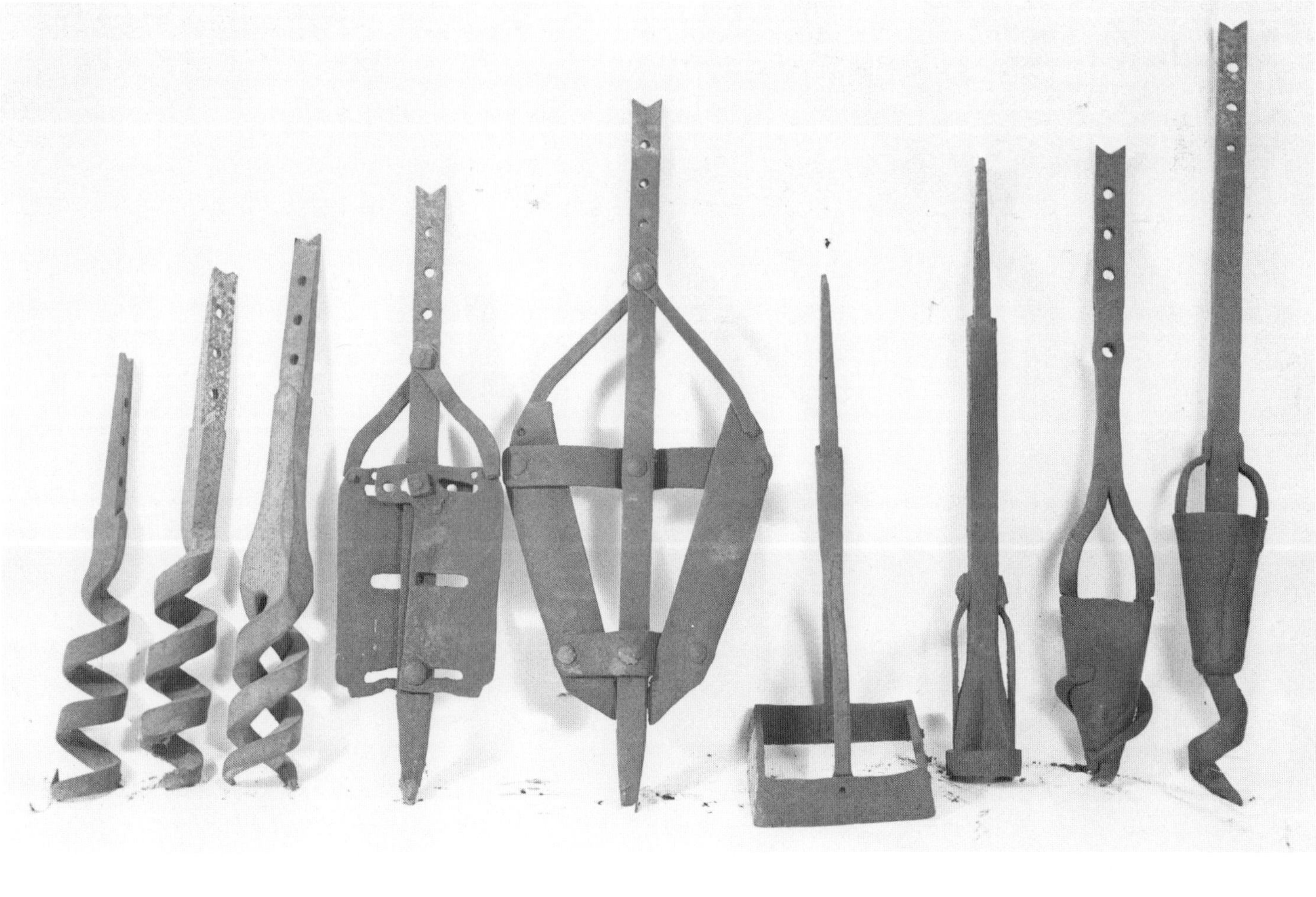

Courtesy Mrs. J. Alphonse Prudhomme

CANE RIVER COUNTRY Louisiana — 111

For boys, football, baseball, and track are much encouraged among outdoor sports. Contests with some of the strongest universities in the South are held. The aim of this work is not to develop winning teams, but to give methods of developing one's own physical nature; to instruct in the art of training others, and to create right ideals in sport and physical training.
Louisiana State Normal School Catalogue, 1911-1912

George Williamson Collection, NSU Archives

Right: Louisiana State Normal football team, 1913
Below: Louisiana State Normal faculty, 1902

George Williamson Collection, NSU Archives

There are one hundred bedrooms, sixty of them arranged for two students each, and four rooms for six students each.

The rooms are provided with white iron and brass beds, moss mattresses, metal washstands, bowls and pitchers, chairs, lamps or electric lights, and fire-places or stoves. Students provide their own pillows, blankets, bed linen, mosquito bars, towels and napkins.

There are nine bath rooms, supplied with full-length porcelain-lined tubs, and hot and cold cistern water.
Louisiana State Normal School Catalogue 1904-1905

Left: Mrs. Donaho in her room in the Matron's Building (Bullard Mansion).
Below: Graduating class, Spring 1902

George Williamson Collection, NSU Archives

George Williamson Collection, NSU Archives

CANE RIVER COUNTRY Louisiana — 113

Right: World War I tank

Robert DeBlieux Collection, NSU Archives

Below: Some Natchitoches men in World War I. Row 1 (left to right): Earl DeBlieux, Earl Freeman, unidentified man. Row 2: unidentified man, Eric DeBlieux, Conly Covington, Gordon Peters, Eugene Gilson, Blount Breazeale, George Himel, Roy Tedlie. Row 3: Bill Payne, Ovid Turpin, Andrew Hargis, Hugh Miller, Adolph Sompayrac, Phonsie Sompayrac, Reginald Prudhomme, Curtis Smith, Sterling LeBlanc, Alex Sompayrac, — Ellzy. Row 4: Archie Breazeale, J. C. Keyser, John T. Pharis, Adolphus Albritton, Hampton Waddell, Isadore Gimbert, D. McLean, Guy Cloutier, Wayne Huckaby, Willie Simpkins, Ollie Gimbert.

Hargis Collection, NSU Archives

The spirit of her women is the spirit of the highest type of American Womanhood. No other city in Louisiana can boast a more notable list of brilliant minds, or brave, heroic citizens, ready for any test. Natchitoches has long been a center of culture and refinement, and of splendid achievement on the part of her women. So naturally the eyes of the whole State will be turned on you, as those who set the pace for the women of our commonwealth.

When we realize the cause and purpose of this war, we know that it can never end until Imperialism is completely overthrown, and the spirit of all nations and kindreds and tongues, shall soar with our own American eagle and from the earth's remotest bounds will echo and re-echo with multitudinous reverberations, the glorious paean, "I am free. I am free."

Caroline Dormon Collection, NSU Archives

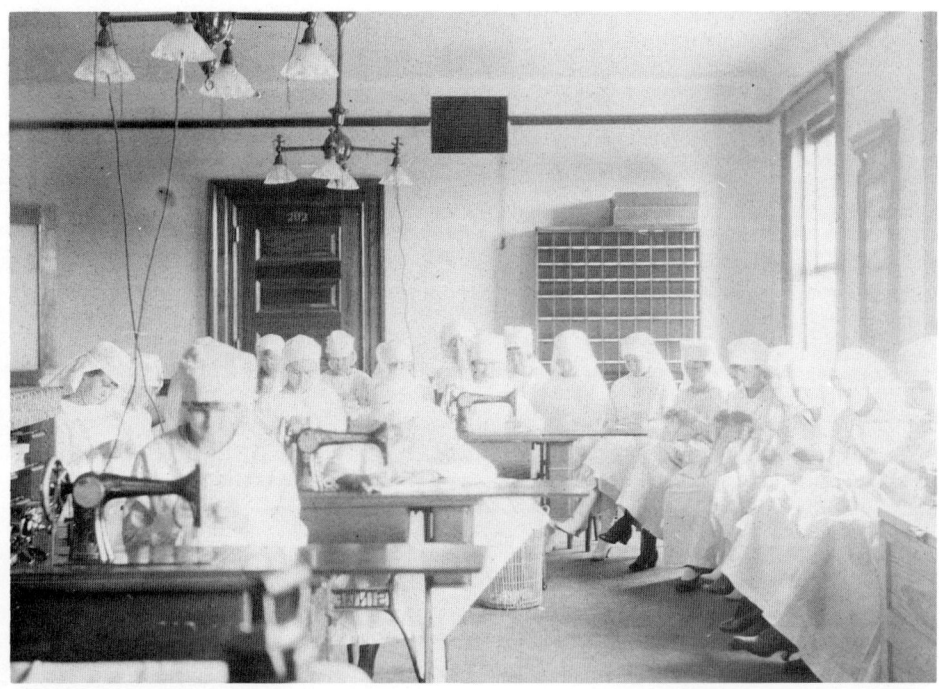

George Williamson Collection, NSU Archives

Left: Women's Red Cross work, Post Office Building, World War I
Below: Natchitoches National Guard, World War I

Giles W. Millspaugh, Jr., Collection, NSU Archives

Melrose Collection, NSU Archives

The aged tree
Sends forth
Small green leaves
To show
Her young heart.
  Mary Land, *Dreams*

Melrose Collection, NSU Archives

Melrose Collection, NSU Archives

The treasure is guarded by a ghostly band, they tell you in all solemnity. Smoke rises from the ground when you thrust your hand down the hole you are digging below the spot where the "Divining rod" circles. Headless horses gallop around. Headless human figures, like smoke-wraiths, holding their ghostly heads in their hands, circle about you, with menacing gestures and eerie sounds. That is the time one of the party must read selected passages from the "devil Book" or the "Sixth and Seventh Books of Moses" lest you come to harm.
  Meigs O. Frost, Melrose Collection, NSU Archives

Melrose Collection, NSU Archives

Melrose Collection, NSU Archives

All three photos: slave quarters, Magnolia Plantation

CANE RIVER COUNTRY Louisiana — 117

Relics to be seen at Little, or Cedar, Lick at Drake's salt dome: wooden pipe used in making salt (note that the wooden pipes are made to fit together)

On the north side, and pretty near the Natchitoches, there is, as is said, a spring of water very salt, running only four leagues. This spring, as it comes out of the earth, forms a little river, which, during the heats, leaves some salt on its banks. And what may render this more credible is, that the country whence it takes its rise contains a great deal of mineral salt, which discovers itself by several springs of salt water, and by two salt lakes, of which I shall presently speak.

Antoine Simon Le Page Du Pratz, *History of Louisiana*, 1774

Photo by Everett Baker for Stanley T. Slaydon's "Present Day Evidence of Past Salt-Making Activities on Drake's Salt Dome," 1973

Left: Evaporating kettle
Below: Wooden pipe

Everett Baker

Everett Baker

CANE RIVER COUNTRY Louisiana — 119

Two views of Natchitoches, early 1890s

Courtesy Library of Congress

Courtesy Library of Congress

I think Cane River must be the crookedest river in the world. It changes its route every hundred yards. It is a wimpling stream of blue water that bubbles up ceaselessly from a million springs. It is generally low enough for boys to wade across, but sometimes it rises high in its tall banks and then it floats such big boats as the Jesse K. Bell. "Before the war" it was always navigable. It has curious banks — this river that was a great river before the war — high yellow bluffs topped with green grass and beneath these, sloping down with a most gentle yielding terrace after terrace, green and plushy, until the edge slips into the river. To see how charming a place the town is one must cross the river and look at it with its proper perspective. It lies along the bluff and up the hillside, and like any other peaceful town, shows its peaceful spires above the encampments of great trees. They are cottonwood trees and they keep up a silver singing all the while like fountains playing in marble basins. The twin towers of the cathedral, not unlike those of Notre Dame, glow darkly red above the trees, and nearby is the steep roof and the exquisitely beautiful belfry, with its red stone slender columns and its grass-bearded crown, of the Episcopal church. The town rambles as every picturesque place ought to do. The streets are narrow, showing the old European force of habit strong on its founders, and the houses are fortresses of masonry, built to last forever and a day. There are wonderful old red brick edifices, standing jamb on the street and built Spanish-wise with the threshold level with the street. The lower story will be surmounted by a broad balcony or porch and even this — like a Chester row — may have a brick pavement worn into shallows by the tread of feet that have been dust these fifty years. Occasionally a broken board shows that the original house is of adobe and has been recently planked over.

Catharine Cole, c. 1889, Melrose Collection, NSU Archives

Lyle Saxon photo, NSU Archives

Zeline Roque's house

Zeline Roque (right) with Juliette on the kitchen porch, 1929

Lyle Saxon photo, NSU Archives

I have known one or two odd specimens of barnyard denizens in the Cane River country. There used to be a fine flock of frizzled chickens at Zeline Roque's ... Sometimes they would have slightly speckled plumage but mostly they were brown and so ruffed and disorderly that one could easily imagine they had just come off second best in an encounter with an electric fan. It was just a detail that some of these hens and roosters had webbed feet.

François Mignon, *Plantation Memo*, 1972

It may appear almost incredible, and yet it is too true, that near seven tenths of Louisiana to the south of the parallel of Natchitoches and Natchez, is either constantly or periodically covered with water. No doubt a considerable proportion of this tract may eventually be redeemed, but not without more labor and expense than is in the power of the present generation to bestow.
    Amos Stoddard, *Sketches, Historical and Descriptive, of Louisiana,* 1812

Robert DeBlieux Collection, NSU Archives

Robert DeBlieux Collection, NSU Archives

All photos, these two pages, show flood waters at Cypress, 1908

Robert DeBlieux Collection, NSU Archives

Robert DeBlieux Collection, NSU Archives

Robert DeBlieux Collection, NSU Archives

... During this period, the African House was used as a lumber room and general plantation catch-all for cast off gear and discarded house furnishings. In the mid 1950s, however, the African House was given a new lease on life when its heterogeneous contents were cleared out, the lower floor converted into an ante-Bellum museum and the upper floor made presentable as a gallery for paintings.
Francois Mignon, *Plantation Memo,* 1972

Melrose Collection, NSU Archives

African House, Melrose

It was upon the store gallery that the black men gathered at night, loafing and "visitin'" together; the deserted building, tight' barred and dark, was their nightly meeting place; it was their club, their refuge from hot cabins full of squalling black children.

Lyle Saxon, "Cane River"

Lyle Saxon photo, NSU Archives

Melrose Plantation store

A little day is mine 'twixt night and night
So short 'tis nearly done —
                    Kate Chopin, "A little Day"

St. "Dennis" Hotel, located on St. Denis Street behind the Live Oak Hotel

Giles W. Millspaugh, Jr., Collection, NSU Archives

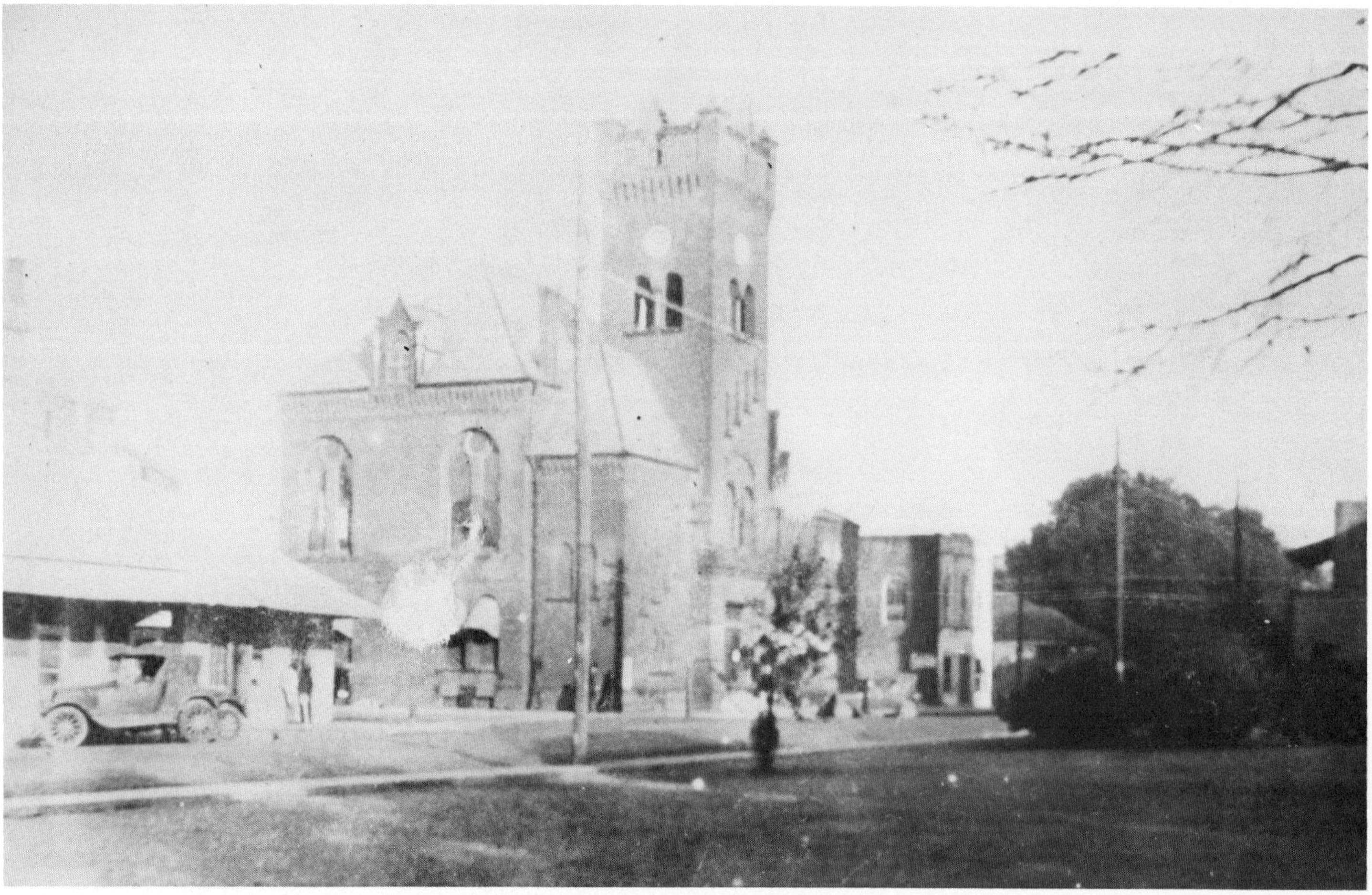

Natchitoches Parish courthouse

Melrose Collection, NSU Archives

126 — CANE RIVER COUNTRY Louisiana

Old courthouse and jail

Robert DeBlieux Collection, NSU Archives

Trades Day crowd on Front Street

Gladys Breazeale Collection, NSU Archives

CANE RIVER COUNTRY Louisiana — 127

First Natchitoches Parish courthouse, torn down in 1888. It was located on the northwest corner of Church and Second Streets.

Judge James W. Jones Collection, NSU Archives

Bishop Polk is here now — an admirable man, I think. I feel some interest in his Church as it is the only Protestant body here. To my surprise I was elected one of the vestrymen at the last election by the congregation. I supposed that only a member could be vestryman. I presume as things go it is an office without duties. If there be such, I know myself too well not to be assured that they will be neglected.
Henry Safford, Natchitoches, 27 April 1857. Safford Collection, NSU Archives

Trinity Episcopal Church, 1891

Some time after the creation of the new diocese, the name of the Cathedral was changed from St. Francis to St. Mary. In December, 1854, the year and the month that the dogma of the Immaculate Conception of the Blessed Virgin Mary was defined, Father P. F. Dicharry, rector of the Cathedral, entered in the registers of the church that he was rector of the "Church of St. Mary of Natchitoches." In 1856, Bishop Martin began the construction of a new Cathedral and it was dedicated under the invocation of the Immaculate Conception.
Roger Baudier, *The Catholic Church in Louisiana*, 1939

Church of the Immaculate Conception

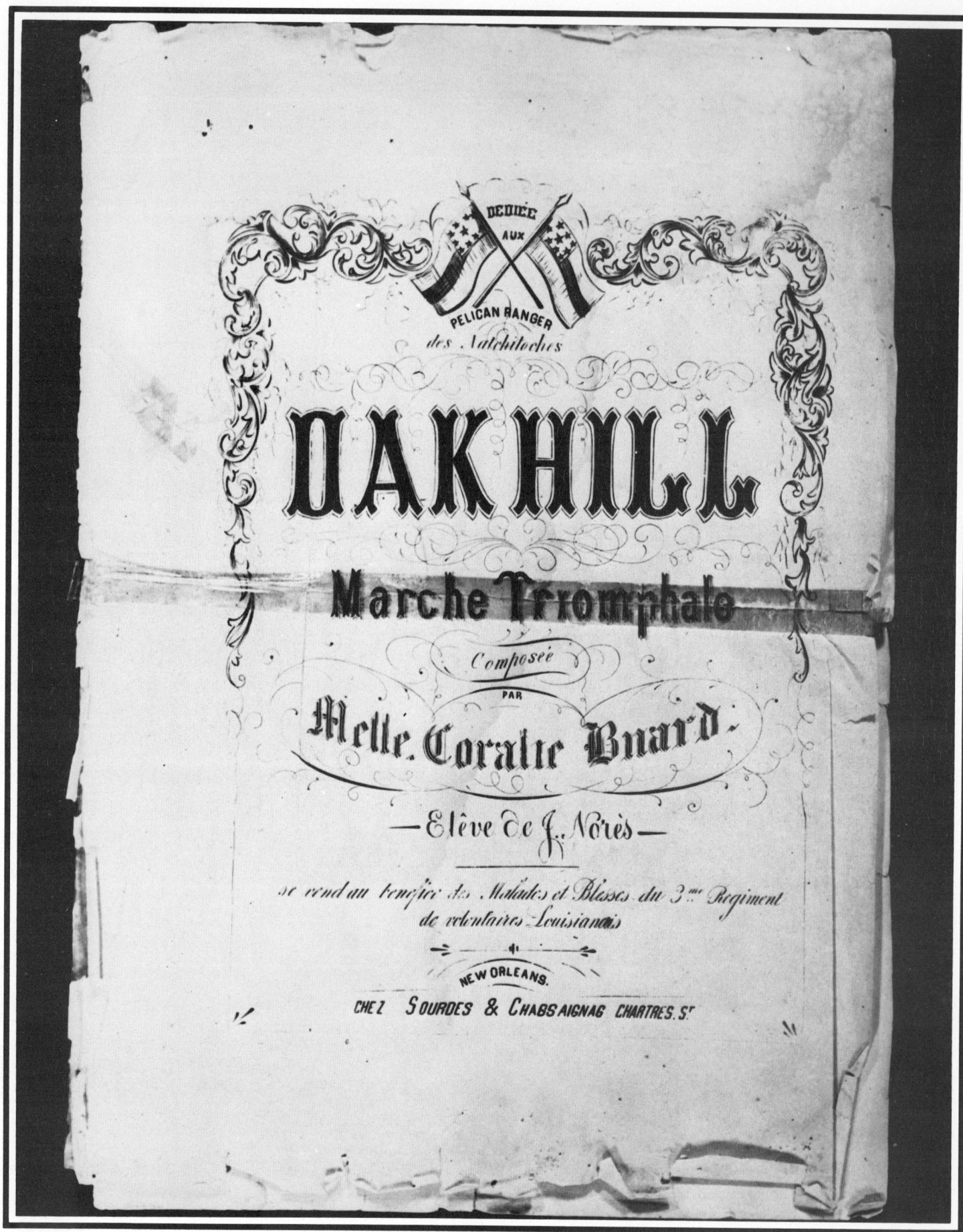

Hyams Collection, NSU Archives

Hyams Collection, NSU Archives

Mlle. Coralie Buard vient de composer un délicieux morceau pour piano, ayant pour titre: Marche Triomphale d'Oak Hill. Cette oeuvre musicale admirablement bien conçue nous a été jouée par le professeur J. Norès, qui doit, en vérité, être fier de son élève. L'harmonie large et puissante de cette marche ou les transitions sont habilement ménagées, la fraicheur du thême musical et l'emsemble parfait de tout le morceau, nous prouvent une fois de plus le talent de son auteur. La Marche Triomphale d'Oak Hill aura du succès dans les salons de la Nelle-Orléans, sa réputation franchira rapidement les limites de Natchitoches.

Natchitoches *Union*, 23 January 1862

Two views of Second Street

Melrose Collection, NSU Archives

Melrose Collection, NSU Archives

Court was in session; along the narrow streets ox-teams were crawling and creaking, filled with niggers and country people "passing" the time of day; now and then some fine old carriage, drawn by satin bays, would permit him a glimpse of ravishing ladies in gay little flowered bonnets; around the hitching posts on the river bank, where umbrella-chinas made pools of shade and the flies circled, drunken and sleepy, the planters had left their horses and mules; and bits of blue and orange and red flashed abroad in the streets.

Ada Jack Carver, "Redbone"

Undated view of Natchitoches

Courtesy Mrs. Dwight Davis

> The village of Natchitoches will always preserve some importance, particularly as it is the usual thoroughfare over land from the settlements east of the Mississippi to the Mexican dominions. A garrison was always kept here by the French and Spaniards, and the United States still maintain one at the same place.
> Amos Stoddard, *Sketches, Historical and Descriptive, of Louisiana,* 1812

1850 plan of Natchitoches

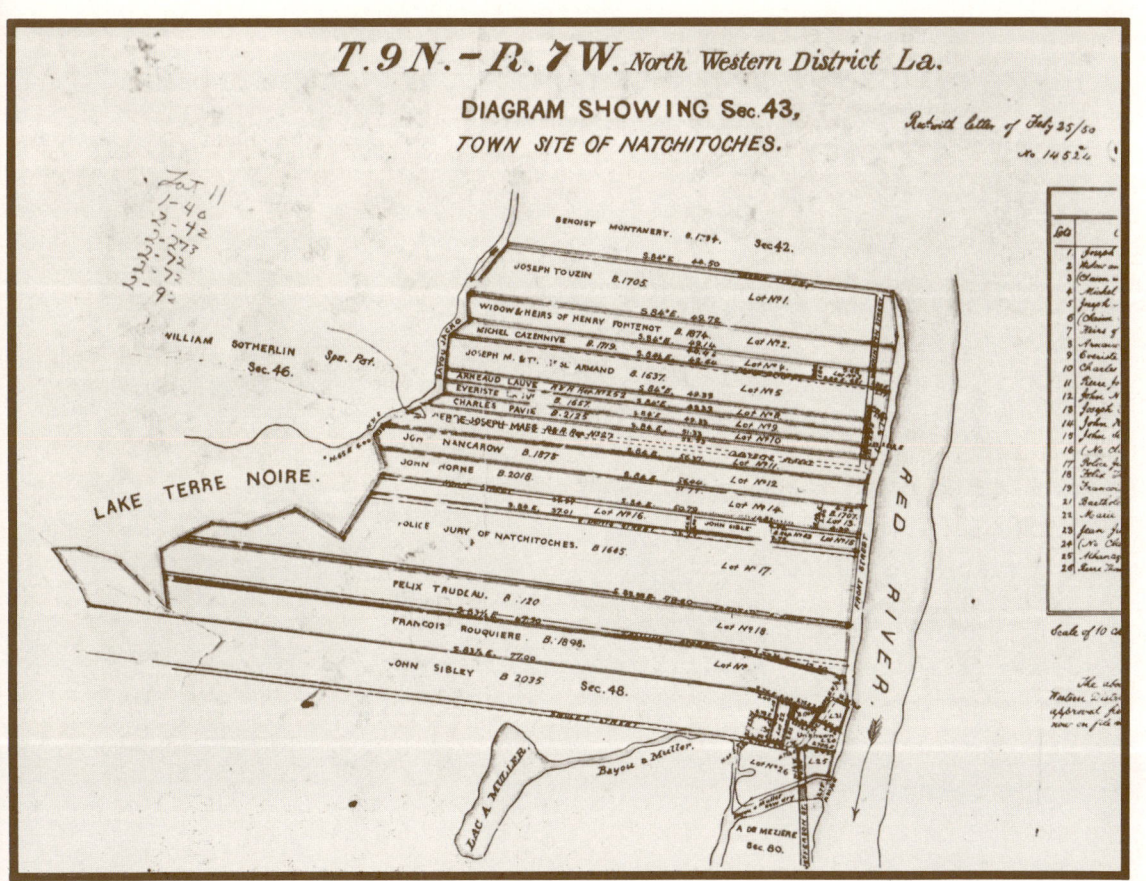

Marshall H. Carver Collection, NSU Archives

CANE RIVER COUNTRY Louisiana — 133

...On spring mornings, the grass along St. Denis Street was shining with the dew, and the birds twittered about their building in the stately elms in front of the old ivy-covered church... Truffles could be found on the old lake bank after a spring shower, and they lent a delicate garnishment to chicken. Artichokes raised their prickly heads, and all the old gardens had their long row of feathery asparagus, when you could pick the tender stalks in the early morning... Those were the times of — but I must desist. Just hearing about all those things, many of which, on any kind of scale, anyway, are but memories these days of conservation. But the magic of cuisine artistry lingers around Natchitoches.

Wynonah Breazeale, "Creole Eats," *The Literary Digest.* 28 June 1919

Riverfront, 1947

Melrose Collection, NSU Archives

Mrs. W.T. Williams' sunken garden on Cane River.

Melrose Collection, NSU Archives

...the flower garden, with its graveled walks and trim parterres, where a tangle of color and perfume were holding high revelry this April morning... Kate Chopin, *Bayou Folk*

Natchitoches City Hall, which served as the L.R.&N. passenger depot from 1910 to 1923

Courtesy B. A. Cohen

> The earth was covered with two inches of snow, as white, as dazzling, as soft as northern snow and a hundred times more beautiful. Snow upon and beneath the moss-draped branches of the forests; snow along the bayou's edges, powdering the low, pointed, thick palmetto growths; white snow and the fields and fields of white cotton bursting from dry bolls. The Natchitoches train sped leisurely through the white, still country, and I longed for some companion to sit beside me who would feel the marvelous and strange beauty of the scene as I did.
>
> Kate Chopin,
> "A December Day in Dixie"

Giles W. Millspaugh, Jr., Collection, NSU Archives; also, Courtesy Mrs. J. Alphonse Prudhomme

Natchitoches Railroad locomotive at the station near the Normal campus.

CANE RIVER COUNTRY Louisiana — 135

Bank of Cloutierville, 1920

Mildred McCoy Collection, NSU Archives

MY NATIVE TOWN
(Written by a schoolgirl, Clemence Benoist, 1888)

Cloutierville is my native place, it is situated on the right bank of the Cane River in the parish of Natchitoches. The little village is not very pretty nor is it at all flourishing, still I love the place for it has always been my home. The chief pursuit of the people around Cloutierville is agriculture. Some of the planters own very large plantations, and they cultivate cotton. Every year hundreds of bales of beautiful white cotton is shipped from the banks of Cane River. Our lands are very rich and some day I suppose this country will be in a flourishing condition. We have but one church in our village and it is a Roman Catholic church. All the people are Creoles except two families. They are Americans and profess the Protestant religion. There is not much trade or commerce carried on in this little place. The climate is very mild and the soil is very fertile. In the spring of the year Cloutierville looks real pretty. Then the flowers are all in bloom, the trees are dressed in green, the little birds sing their gay songs and little old Cloutierville looks pretty and festive.

Melrose Collection, NSU Archives

... the large building occupied by the Red River Land Company and the Natchitoches Railroad. This was formerly the residence of Lecomte, so well known through the whole country, and abroad, as the owner of the celebrated racing horse of the same name. In the background loom up the spires of numerous churches for which, and also its schools, Natchitoches is justly noted.
The South Illustrated, June 1887.

Left: Old Lecomte Building, Southwest corner of Front and Church Streets.
Below: Lecomte Building, Southwest corner of Front and Church Streets.

Giles W. Millspaugh, Jr., Collection, NSU Archives

Melrose Collection, NSU Archives

When first we gathered in a class,
Called forth by the Normal bell,
We felt we could almost conquer the
   earth
If we took for our maxim: "Do Well!"

But as the days went swiftly by
Things were not learned to the letter;
Our monthly slips brought forth
   many a sigh —
Each silently vowed to "Do Better!"

Tho' times go on from worse to worse —
Each month beats all the rest —
We're not complaining of lessons at all —
We simply strive to "Do Best!"
Potpourri, 1911

Sketch of Guardia Hall entrance by Velma C. Hargis

Hargis Collection, NSU Archives

I tell you now in mornful numbers,
   Practice teaching's a hideous dream,
For we have no time to slumber
   And things are worse than they seem.
. . .
Critic teachers that remind us,
   "Lack of 'Subject-matter' is a heinous crime"
So departing we leave behind us
   Failures on the sands of time.
        Potpourri, 1909

Model School (Lab School) and Guardia Hall

George Williamson Collection, NSU Archives

Melrose Collection, NSU Archives

**Louisiana State Normal School
Graduating Class, 1892**
Back row (left to right): Maggie McBride, Miss Gregg, Mr. Ling (teacher), Lisa Payne, Kate Lea Trichel, Bessie Harwell. Middle row: Laura Tauzin, Bessie McKitrick, Mamie Cross, Mathilde Greneaux, Maggie Cade. Front row: Emma Quimby, Cammie Garrett, Lizzie Barrett, Effie Dalzell, Mollie Kearney

Melrose Collection, NSU Archives

Normal Students 1890

1. May Smith (Sanders)
2. Mary Cross
3. Mattie Hyde
4. Anna Hill
5. Annie Burris
6. Annie Brandon
7. Sallie Spencer
8. Celeste Wales
9. Lessie Bonham
10. Maggie Ezell
11. Elodie Heblouin
12. Sallie Firmiss
13. Lulu Weiland
14. Mary Belle Lane
15. Hugh D. McLaurin
16. Edna Montgomery
17. May Stidham
18. Emma Dawkins
19. Louise Honeycutt
20. Addie Butler
21. Bessie Munday
22. Ida Milling
23. Lizzie Alexander
24. Cammie Garrett
25. Emma Dollerhyde
26. Mary Washington
27. Julie Dale
28. Emma Oswalt
29. Lizzie Barrett
30. Amelia Gaulden
31. Zoe Garig
32. Alma Mausur
33. Stella Schorten

Children and teacher. Standing (left to right): Robert Hollingsworth, Louise Gallion, Lizzie Bloodworth, Abe Bath. Sitting: Bessie Pierson, Miss May Huey (teacher), Lee Walmsley. On floor: Ann Kearney, ( ) Levy, Ethel Bullard, ( ). Two boys: Milton Trichel, Joseph Bath

Antebellum convent school

The House of the Brides

Clem P. Binnings, "Natchitoches," Louisiana Collection, Watson Library, NSU

Stephens house (St. Clair plantation house)

Clem P. Binnings, "Natchitoches," Louisiana Collection, Watson Library, NSU

Eclipse Brass Band

Giles W. Millspaugh, Jr., Collection, NSU Archives

Courtesy Mrs. J. Alphonse Prudhomme

Opening of the Bermuda, La., bridge

A scene in the American Cemetery, 1979

Courtesy B. A. Cohen

St. Denis tree, 1927
The St. Denis tree stands near the center of the American grave-yard in the southern part of Natchitoches; on the crest of the hill just as it begins to slope toward the Cane Lake. There it has stood according to tradition, where St. Denis planted it more than 100 years ago. This indeed we do not know, and to my mind is obvious, but that it has stood guard over the dead for many years and that its roots have gone deep into the earth and taken up the substance of the bodies of those that sleep about it, and that the leaves and branches that we see waving so gracefully in the breezes, are a part of the people that once walked upon the banks of the lakes and admired other trees as we do this one, is utmost in my mind.

A. Babb, "My Sketch Book"

The Normal columns

Gladys Breazeale Collection, NSU Archives

The first St. Mary's Academy, date undetermined

Giles W. Millspaugh, Jr., Collection, NSU Archives

Two views of the school boat *Pearl*

Courtesy Mrs. C. C. Dethloff

Courtesy Mrs. J. C. Perot

CANE RIVER COUNTRY Louisiana — 149

Boyd Hall, Louisiana State Normal School, ready for commencement

George Williamson Collection, NSU Archives

Boyd Hall is a large frame building erected in 1895, under the administration of Col. Thos. D. Boyd. During the summer of 1912 the building was moved to a position near the power house and parallel to the main building, the change having been made to afford a proper location for the new practice school building.

Boyd Hall is now used exclusively for academic purposes. On the first floor are found the home economics department, the chemistry classroom and laboratory, classrooms for the department of rural training, and several offices. The second floor contains a large auditorium, now used as a gymnasium, and the biological classroom and laboratory. On the third floor are found the physics classroom and laboratory.

Louisiana State Normal College catalog, 1921

The classes are held in old school houses and churches about the parish. It brings tears to ones eyes to go into a class room and see the pupils, young and old, struggling to get that which should have been their right in youth. The men work in the field all day and go home and clean up and walk for miles to the school and struggle for two or three hours by lamp light, trying to learn to read and write. Some of them are so tired that they fall asleep over their books. When people are that anxious to learn they certainly should not be denied the chance.

       Mildred Wells, Parish
       Director of Relief, 1930s

Melrose Collection, NSU Archives

Melrose Collection, NSU Archives

Emergency Relief Administration, adult education classes, 1934

Melrose Collection, NSU Archives

CANE RIVER COUNTRY Louisiana — 151

Teachers of Natchitoches Parish, December 1913, at a teachers' convention, Natchitoches Post Office.

Giles W. Millspaugh, Jr., Collection, NSU Archives

Group at Clear Lake, Natchitoches Parish, about 1904. Boys (left to right) Henry Lattier, unidentified person. Girls (left to right) Addie Rachal, Chloe Lattier, Ida Lattier, Emma Gallien

Courtesy Mrs. Marie Stroud

View of the Louisiana State Normal School

George Williamson Collection, NSU Archives

April 5th, 1917
My dear Sir; —

I regret very much to have to send Miss Lizzie home. I find that on a recent occasion when I was called to Baton Rouge on business she and another girl went out auto riding with two men from town. This was a violation of one of our most rigid rules. It is a lapse of good conduct that we cannot tolerate in a big institution where more than 500 girls live.

I feel that I am doing the best thing that I can for Miss Lizzie by returning her to her home where her parents can look after her with more care, attention and solicitude than is possible in large boarding school.

Miss Lizzie will leave from Natchitoches at 8 o'clock Friday morning . . .
Yours very truly,

V. L. Roy

[University Archives, NSU]

Courtesy Don Sepulvado

Courtesy Don Supulvado

Above left: Warren Easton Hall; above right: Caldwell Hall; left: "the columns" and old Russell Library, all on the campus at Northwestern State University.

Courtesy Don Supulvado

CANE RIVER COUNTRY Louisiana — 155

Right: modern Watson Library, Northwestern State University.
Below: sundial in the old Northwestern quadrangle.

Courtesy Don Sepulvado

Courtesy Don Sepulvado

Courtesy The Service League of Natchitoches, Inc. ©Cane River Cuisine 1974; photo by John C. Guillet

On the porch at the H. C. Taylor home.

Courtesy Robert Allen

Courtesy Tommy G. Johnson

Courtesy Dixie Whittington

158 — CANE RIVER COUNTRY Louisiana

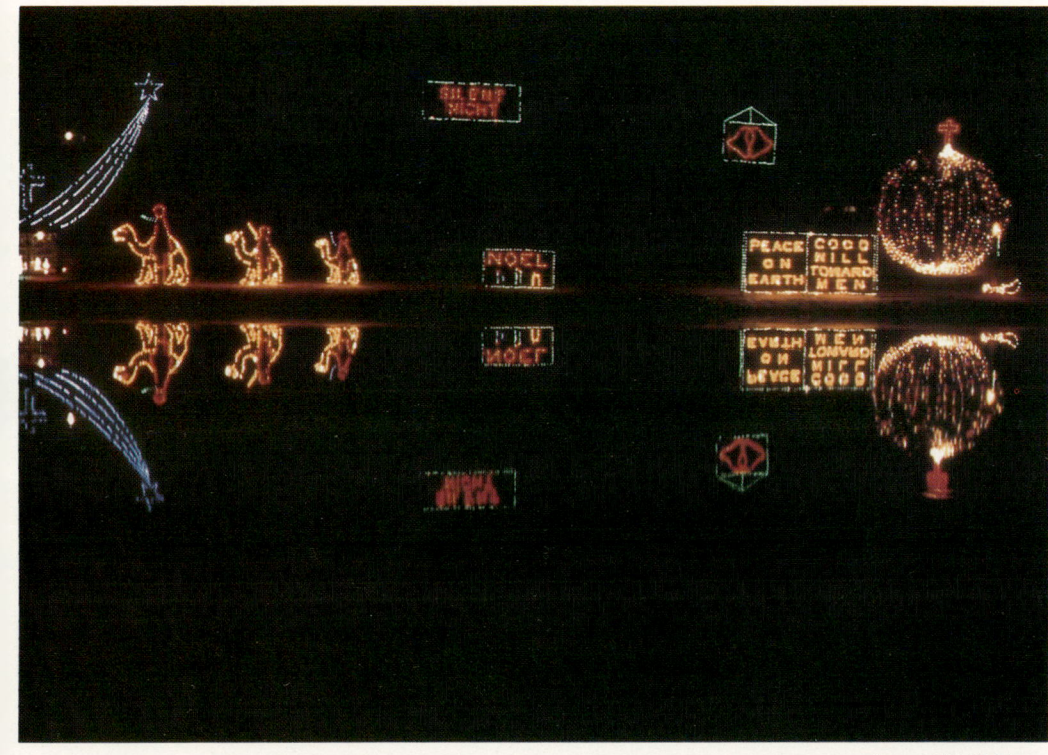

The Christmas season in Natchitoches — Opposite page, top left: Santa on window of NSU Student Union; a burst of fireworks is next to Santa, and Front Street under Christmas lights are below him. At left are the three wise men and signs in lights on Cane River. Below, the Church Street bridge Christmas lights are reflected in Cane River.

Courtesy Dixie Whittington

Courtesy Tommy G. Johnson

CANE RIVER COUNTRY Louisiana — 159

Alvin DeBlieux house.

Courtesy B. A. Cohen

Willow Plantation house, watercolor by Sompayrac Willard

Courtesy Irma Sompayrac Willard

CANE RIVER COUNTRY Louisiana — 161

Courtesy Louisiana Outdoor Drama Association (LODA)

Scenes on these two pages are of stage action in "Louisiana Cavalier", an amphitheatre production at Grand Ecore by the Louisiana Outdoor Drama Association (LODA).

Courtesy Louisiana Outdoor Drama Association (LODA)

162 — CANE RIVER COUNTRY Louisiana

Courtesy Louisiana Outdoor Drama Association (LODA)

Courtesy Louisiana Outdoor Dance Association (LODA)

Courtesy Louisiana Outdoor Drama Association (LODA)

CANE RIVER COUNTRY Louisiana — 163

Courtesy Gayla Adams-Miller

Courtesy Tommy G. Johnson

164 — CANE RIVER COUNTRY Louisiana

Courtesy Tommy G. Johnson

Opposite page, top: a sunrise across Cane River; below: a sunset on Sibley Lake. Left: remnants of a bousillage chimney. Below: a house of bousillage construction.

Courtesy Adrian's Photography

The Henry C. Gahagan house.

Courtesy B. A. Cohen

166 — CANE RIVER COUNTRY Louisiana

The George L. Celles house.

Courtesy B. A. Cohen

The Armelia Rachal house, Melrose.

Courtesy Adrian's Photography

The John Taylor house.

Courtesy B. A. Cohen

Sunset on Cane River

Courtesy The Service League of Natchitoches, Inc., © *Cane River Cuisine 1974*; photo by John C. Guillet.

Girls Dormitory

A. A. Fredericks Collection, NSU Archives

NSU Archives

June 15, 1925
Dear Mr. Roy: We are ready to conduct the experiment with Coca Cola...
    V.E. Cook
    Crystal Ice & Bottling Co.

June 16, 1925
Dear Mrs. Hereford: The Coca Cola people have been worrying me for about 12 years because I bar Coca Cola from the campus. Recently, they sent their chemist from St. Louis to convince me that Coca Cola is not half as harmful as coffee drunk in moderation. However, I agreed with Mr. Cook to make a test. Our plan is to furnish one of the dormitories with a few cases of pop after study hours and watch the effects. Please let me know what you think of this plan.
    V. L. Roy

June 27, 1925
My Dear Mr. Roy: It is needless to say, we are quite gratified at the results of the Coca Cola test conducted in Cottage Three last Wednesday Evening...
    V. E. Cook
    Crystal Ice & Bottling Co.

Two views of "Rose Lawn", the J. H. Williams house.

"ROSE LAWN"

I know a garden, tho the hands
   That tended it are gone,
The sweet, old-fashioned flowers that
   Once flourished there, live on;
Still daffodils and crocus star
   The cedar's deepest shade,
And hyacinths remember where
   The winding paths were laid.

Ah, loved ones gone! My heart is like
   A garden long bereft,
Where only sturdy, long-lived things
   (The sweetest too) are left,
For thoughts of you, like daffodils,
   Still light my deepest gloom.
And down the paths of memory
   Are hyacinths in bloom.

      Lillian Hall Trichel,
      Dormon Collection, NSU Archives

Melrose Collection, NSU Archives

Robert DeBlieux Collection, NSU Archives

Immediately after his consecration, Bishop Martin set to work. He had before him a population of 25,000 souls scattered over an area of 22,000 square miles. His diocese extended from the 31st degree of latitude north to the Arkansas state line and from the Sabine River to the Mississippi River. In this vast territory, he had four priests and seven churches...

Roger Baudier, *The Catholic Church in Louisiana,* 1939

Left: Catholic rectory, Natchitoches [Historic District]
Below left: the bishop's house [Historic District]
Below right: Bishop Martin

Courtesy B. A. Cohen

Courtesy B. A. Cohen

Courtesy B. A. Cohen

Tauzin-Wells house [Historic District]

Giles W. Millspaugh, Jr., Collection, NSU Archives

About four hundred miles from the mouth of the Red River, is found, as one goes upstream, the settlement of Natchitoches. It counts twelve or thirteen hundred inhabitants. They raise profitably cotton, maize, rice, and tobacco. The products of that place pass as the best of North America. Also the king of Spain bought of all the proprietors at a suitable price, but he has been cheated so often, that he has ceased to buy there for several years. Consequently agriculture there has almost entirely ceased. Besides those products, a large part of the inhabitants trade with the Indian nations surrounding them. The peltries resulting from the trade are very inferior in quality to those of the northern provinces. Through that small settlement pass the merchants or adventurers who engage in contraband trade in Mexico. Spain keeps a garrison of sixty men there under command of a captain.

Perrin Du Lac, *Voyage*, 1805

Pierre Evariste Bossier, who died 24 April 1844

Courtesy Don Sepulvado

James Ryder Randall, the author of "Maryland! My Maryland!" wrote the following dirge upon learning of the death of Placide Bossier, a college friend at Georgetown University. Placide Bossier, private, Company G, Third Regiment (Pelican Rangers), Louisiana Infantry, was killed in action, August 10, 1861, at the battle of Oak Hill, Mo.

> Ah, friend! in the tender college time
> No evil deed could stain thee,
> And now, 'mid the combat's iron chime
> In purity they've slain thee.
> *Sans peur et sans reproche* to live,
> *Sans peur* the foe defying,
> *Sans peur et sans reproche* we give
> Thy epitaph when dying.

Hyams Collection, NSU Archives

Keator house, Bermuda, La., 1903

Courtesy Mrs. J. Alphonse Prudhomme

Left to right: J. T. Keator, M.D.; Cecile Prudhomme; Kitten (Kate Keator); Emile Prudhomme; Mae (Mary Keator); Rose M. Keator; J. E. Keator, M.D.; P. Emanuel Prudhomme holding Meda Keator

Courtesy Mrs. J. Alphonse Prudhomme

Courtesy Mrs. Alexander Andrews

Every day gentle showers watered the fields. The cotton grew tall and green; banana trees unfurled their large translucent leaves in the garden before the door, and the dark polished leaves of the magnolia glittered like metal. There were singing birds in each tree and the air was filled with the droning of bees and the shrilling of locusts. Hot summer, old hot summer had come.

Lyle Saxon, *Children of Strangers*

John S. Kyser Collection, NSU Archives

Two views of the Russell house, formerly standing on Second Street

Late Senator Phanor Breazeale's home on North Front Street, 1927

Melrose Collection, NSU Archives

The morning of February 22nd [1927] was a pretty, bright day, more like April than February. I had made my usual round on the job, and resolved to take a stroll . . . I turned North on Front St. I was looking at the quaint old building with its window blinds and comparing it with the one next to it. Just then a big car passed and turned in the driveway ahead of me; I was approaching Ex Senator Breazeale's home; a lady stepped out of the car and walked back meeting me; it was Miss Marie Breazeale. She said that she and Mrs. Bath were going in about an hour to plant some trees on the new sanitarium grounds and invited me to go with them.

A. Babb, "Sketch Book"

Baptiste passed through lanes that were dense with Cherokee roses, on down the road through the frenzied bloom of black-eyed Susan and bitterweed. And where the sinuous river begins to work its magic he saw the town, already asleep with summer. On the edge of the commons the breath of sweet-olive rushed at his lips like a kiss; and it is here that the road grows into a street, with quaint little sociable houses that squat on the sidewalk like children.

Ada Carver, "Redbone"

Melrose Collection, NSU Archives

Tucker House, originally called St. Amant house where parish library now stands

Jean Baptiste Metoyer house

Melrose Collection, NSU Archives

After passing this [River Cane] settlement ... the river divides again, forming another island of about thirty miles in length, and from two to four in breadth, called the *Isle Brevel,* after a reputable old man now living in it, who first settled it. This island is sub-divided by a bayou that communicates from one river to the other, called also Bayou Brevel. The middle division of the river, is called *Little* river, and it is thickly settled, and is the boat channel; the westward division of the river is called False river, is navigable, but not settled, the banks are too low; it passes through a lake called Lac Occassa.
John Sibley, Natchitoches, 10th April 1805, in *Travels in Interior America,* 1807

J. P. Breda house, built 1859 above Breda Lake

Melrose Collection, NSU Archives

Alex. P. Breda, Dr. Medecin, Gradué à l'Université de la Louisane Setant Associé, pour la pratique de la Médecine, avec le Dr. BREDA offre ses services aux habitants de Natchitoches et des environs.
Résidence chez de Dr. P. Breda.

April 1861, Natchitoches newspaper clipping

The undersigned Mail Contractors, on the route from Shreveport to Natchitoches have so arranged the stands on the route that the Coaches will hereafter meet in Mansfield. The arrivals and Departures are permanently arranged as follows:

Arrivals		Departures	
Mondays,	5 P.M.	Tuesdays,	3 A.M.
Thursdays,	do.	Fridays,	do.
Saturdays,	do.	Sundays,	do.

They have succeeded in forming a connection with the line through to the mouth of Red River. Persons traveling on this route will meet with no delay. The time required in making a trip from Shreveport to the mouth of Red River will be four days lying over one night at Mansfield. For comfort and speed, this line is unsurpassed by any in the Western States. Good accommodations all the way through. The stand in Mansfield is at the De Soto Hotel. The Proprietor of which (Joel A. Carrell,) is authorized to act as our way agent at this place.
Reesides, Smead, & Co.
August the 16th 1856

Clipping from *DeSoto Columbia*
Melrose Collection, NSU Archives

Courtesy B. A. Cohen

Courtesy B. A. Cohen

**Top: Exchange Bank
Center: City Bank
Right: Peoples Band**

Courtesy B. A. Cohen

Melrose Collection, NSU Archives

Old François Roubieu homestead was settled and surveyed in 1808 by François Roubieu a native of Bordeaux, France. My grandmother Ausite Roubieu moved to her residence on Amulet St. in the town of Natchitoches after my grandfather's death. I moved on Cane river to the old François Roubieu Homestead in 1877 and I named the plantation "Reform Plantation." The post office was Pecan P.O. and I was Postmaster.

Thos. J. Flanner, 1930, Melrose Collection, NSU Archives

Courtesy B. A. Cohen

Tessier Plantation, "Navajo," on Red River

Melrose Collection, NSU Archives

A dozen rods or more from the Red River bank stood the dwelling house, and nowhere upon the plantation had time touched so sadly as here. The steep, black, moss-covered roof sat like an extinguisher above the eight large rooms that it covered, and had come to do its office so poorly that no more than half of these were habitable when the rain fell. Perhaps the live oaks made too thick and close a shelter about it. The verandas were long and broad and inviting; but it was well to know that the brick pillar was crumbling away under one corner, that the railing was insecure at another, and that still another had long ago been condemned as unsafe.

Kate Chopin, *Bayou Folk*

Willow Plantation

Melrose Collection, NSU Archives

Willow Plantation, near Grand Ecore. Built by Alexandre Louis DeBlieux who came over to Louisiana with his father, from Provence, France. Built prior to the Civil War. After being disabled in the war, Pierre Lestan Prud'homme, author of the Young Man's Dairy of 1850-1853, spent his last days here with his sister, Mrs. E. Valery DeBlieux and her family.
Irma Sompayrac Willard

This house on the corner of Washington Avenue and Pavie Street is one of the older landmarks of the City and has a most interesting history. It is now [1938] about one hundred and thirty-two years old and the four large magnolia trees in front of it are probably one hundred years of age. The building is three stories high, the lower and upper stories having a ceiling height of eight feet and the middle story a little over thirteen. The lower floor is brick and the sills, beams, studding and rafters of the building are of hand-hewn cypress. Some of the pieces are forty feet long. The middle story is plastered. There are two large sundried brick chimneys with open fireplaces on the first and second stories.

Charles C. Carroll, "The Old Lauve House"

Melrose Collection, NSU Archives

Two views of the Carroll Lauve house known as The Magnolias [Historic District]

Courtesy B. A. Cohen

Three views of the Benjamin Metoyer town house with the Buard town house in the background of two views [Historic District]

CANE RIVER COUNTRY Louisiana — 187

Two views of Laureate House, also known as the Voiers, Chaplain, and Dunckleman house [Historic District]

Robert DeBlieux Collection, NSU Archives

Melrose Collection, NSU Archives

Levy house [Historic District]

Melrose Collection, NSU Archives

∴ Pledges made in the flush of joy, and in the full tide of prosperity, when the heart is buoyant with hope, may be forgotten or overlooked, but when the clouds and storms of adversity are upon us, and the heart swells with grief and sorrow, the pledges uttered in such a moment are irrevocably fixed, and death alone can prevent their fulfilment.

    From the reply of Captain William M. Levy, 1861, upon the occasion of the presentation of the flag to the Lecomte Guards, Natchitoches.

Two views of the "The Old Brick House," Ackel-Dranguet house, built 1820 [Historic District]

Melrose Collection, NSU Archives

Courtesy B. A. Cohen

Robert DeBlieux Collection, NSU Archives

Suddath house, 1909

Phillips house, 1909

Robert DeBlieux Collection, NSU Archives

CANE RIVER COUNTRY Louisiana — 191

The discipline of the Normal Boarding Club is in the hands of the President of the institution and the matron in charge of the dormitories; and every proper care is exercised in supervising and directing the young men and women of the school. The rules necessary to govern so large a body of young people are more stringent than those found in the home. Accordingly, no student is permitted to spend the night away from the dormitories; visiting in town requires a special permit; and when students go out on excursions to the woods, they are accompanied by members of the faculty.
State Normal School Catalog, 1914-1915

Robert DeBlieux Collection, NSU Archives

East Hall, the New Dormitory, 1890s

Studies I love,
Critique I love,
Plans I love, I say;
Teaching I love with all my heart,
And boys I cast away.
Potpourri, 1911

The Model School includes eight grades and high school, ten rooms, with thirty-five pupils to each room. It aims to exemplify the entire course of study prescribed for the public schools of Louisiana, and to illustrate the best teaching under the best conditions.

For two half-hour periods each day, the lessons are given by students in the fourth year of the normal course; these lessons are prepared and given under direction and supervision of the training teacher and the grade teachers, and no lesson can be given before it has been examined and approved by them.
Louisiana State Normal School Catalog, 1907-1908

George Williamson Collection, NSU Archives

The Model School

Nothing to get but lessons,
   Nowhere to go but to school;
Nothing to see but girls,
   Nothing to keep but the rule.

Nothing to drink but water,
   Nothing to eat but food;
Nothing to feel but homesickness,
   Nothing to be but good.

Nothing to sing but choruses,
   Nothing to teach but kids;
Nothing to do but study —
   Nothing but what's been did.

Nothing is ever different,
   And so our club life goes;
Nothing at all but a Normal girl
   Can understand these woes.

Potpourri, 1911

Two 1909 views of the Louis Dupleix house

Robert DeBlieux Collection, NSU Archives

Robert DeBlieux Collection, NSU Archives

Hidden Hill Plantation

Harriet Beecher Stowe Collection, NSU Archives

It was a wild, forsaken road, now winding through dreary pine barrens, where the wind whispered mournfully, and now over log causeways, through long cypress swamps, the doleful trees rising out of the slimy, spongy ground, hung with long wreaths of funeral black moss, while ever and anon the loathsome form of the moccasin snake might be seen sliding among broken stumps and shattered branches that lay here and there, rotting in the water.

The place had that ragged, forlorn appearance, which is always produced by the evidence that the care of the former owner has been left to go to utter decay.

What was once a smooth-shaven lawn before the house, dotted here and there with ornamental shrubs, was now covered with frowsy tangled grass, with horseposts set up, here and there, in it, where the turf was stamped away, and the ground littered with broken pails, cobs of corn, and other slovenly remains. Here and there a mildewed jessamine or honeysuckle hung raggedly from some ornamental support, which had been pushed to one side by being used as a horse-post. What once was a large garden was now all grown over with weeds, through which, here and there, some solitary exotic reared its forsaken head. What had been a conservatory had now no window shades, and on the mouldering shelves stood some dry, forsaken flower pots, with sticks in them, whose dried leaves showed they had once been plants.

The wagon rolled up a weedy gravel walk, under a noble avenue of China trees, whose graceful forms and ever springing foliage seemed to be the only things there that neglect could not daunt or alter — like noble spirits, so deeply rooted in goodness, as to flourish and grow stronger amid discouragement and decay.

Harriet Beecher Stowe, *Uncle Tom's Cabin*

Marco house

Melrose Collection, NSU Archives

The Marco house was built by Nicola Gratia in the 1820s or 1830s. "The property owned by Mr. Givanovich embraces very much more than the old Nicola Gratia property. I find of record a sale made by Nicola Gratia to Marco Givanovich on May 29, 1860, comprising what was known as the Home Place situated on Cane River containing in the aggregate 5740 acres together with some forty or fifty slaves and a large number of mules and farming implements, etc. The sale was on credit terms and as you will note it was made just prior to the beginning of the Civil War. I find that after the war some time in '68 the notes given for the purchase price were duly cancelled as having been paid by Mr. Marco Givanovich."

Phanor Breazeale to Mrs. Cammie Henry

Prudhomme-Rouquier house (The Service League of Natichitoches house) [Historic District]

Melrose Collection, NSU Archives

CANE RIVER COUNTRY Louisiana — 197

Magnolia Plantation

Courtesy B. A. Cohen

Old Chamard house [Historic District]

Courtesy Robert Smith, architect

Cunningham law office [Historic District]

District Judges, 1892 to the present:

1892-1896	James Andrews	1930-1940	James W. Jones Jr.
1895-1896	A. V. Coco	1940-1942	special judges
1896-1899	E. G. Hunter	1942-1966	Laurie Paul Stephens
1898-1899	E. North Cullom Jr.	1960-1972	Julian E. Bailes
1899-1900	A. J. Lafargue	1966-present	Richard B. Williams
1900-1907	C. V. Porter	1972-present	W. Peyton Cunningham Jr.
1907-1912	Samuel J. Henry		
1912-1920	W. T. Cunningham		
1920-1924	James W. Jones Jr.		
1924-1930	John F. Stephens		

Judge R. B. Williams, "The History of the Judiciary of Natchitoches Parish," *The Natchitoches Genealogist* (April 1978)

Spiral stairway

John S. Kyser Collection, NSU Archives

Spiral stairway and balcony

Courtesy B. A. Cohen

CANE RIVER COUNTRY Louisiana — 201

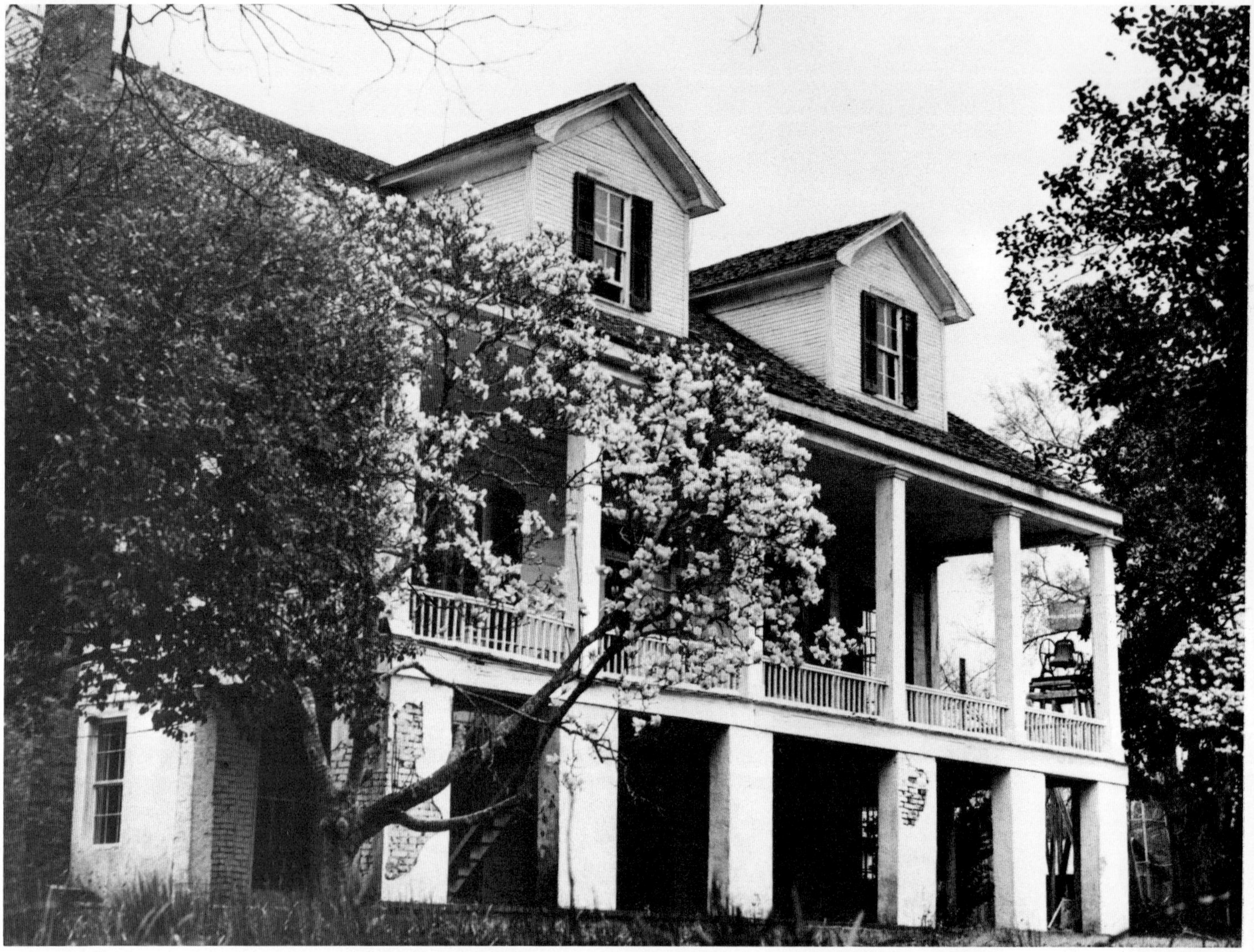

Courtesy B. A. Cohen

Two views of St. Maurice Plantation house, St. Maurice, La.

Courtesy B. A. Cohen

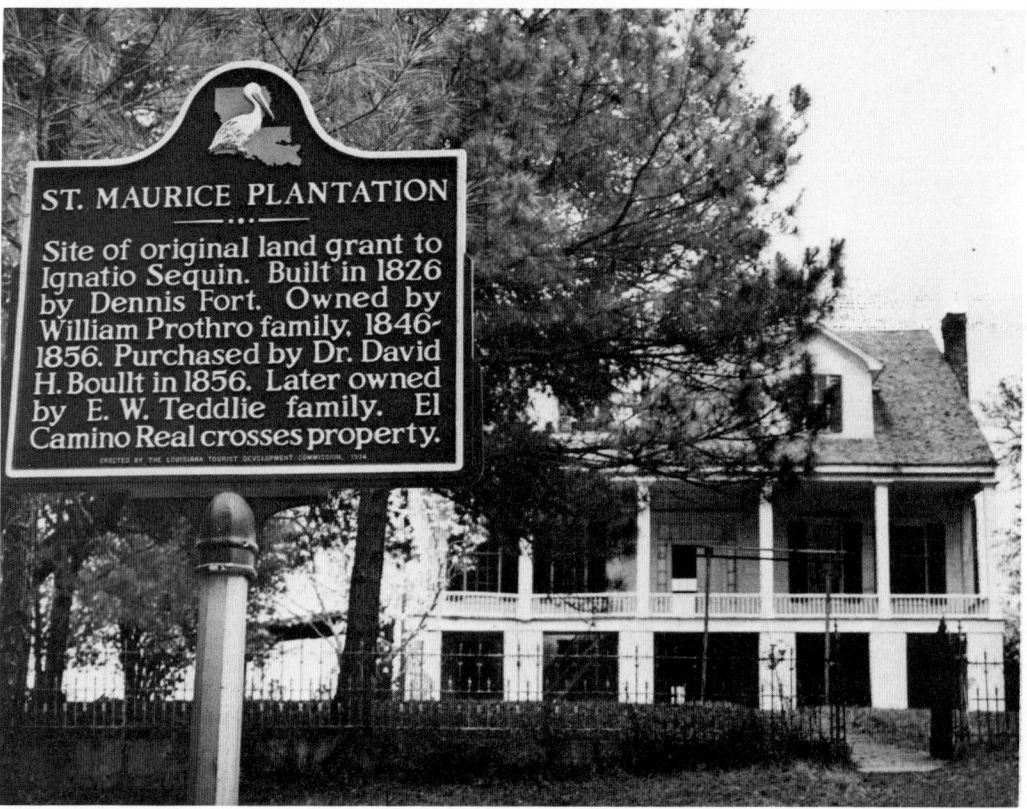

Tante Huppé house [Historic District]

Courtesy B. A. Cohen

Proclamation!

WHEREAS, the Almighty God in his infinite wisdom has taken from our midst one of his beloved servants, the Right Reverend Anthony Piegay, and

WHEREAS, Father Piegay has labored in this community with his flock for over fifty-two years; and

WHEREAS, this minister of God has enjoyed the love, respect and admiration of all the people of this community, regardless of creed; and

WHEREAS, such a character as this is entitled to whatever small tribute of respect and admiration can be shown at a time like this,

NOW THEREFORE, I, Edwin L. McClung, Jr., in my official capacity as Mayor of the City of Natchitoches, do hereby call upon the citizens of Natchitoches to pause in their endeavors and to suspend the operation of their places of business during the hours of the funeral services which will be held at the Church of the Immaculate Conception from ten to twelve o'clock on the morning of Friday, October 20th.

In testimony whereof, I hereunto affix my signature at Natchitoches, Louisiana, this 18th day of October, in the year Nineteen Hundred Thirty Nine.

EDWIN L. McCLUNG, Jr.
Mayor

Melrose Collection, NSU Archives

Right: Mayor's Proclamation about Father Piegay's funeral
Below left: John Murphy
Below right: Dr. Milton Dunn

Courtesy Mrs. William Nolan

Melrose Collection, NSU Archives

Midwife, "Aunt" Marie

Courtesy Mrs. Hilda Perini Heim

Mrs. Cammie Garrett Henry

Courtesy Joseph (Pat) Henry, Jr.

When steamboat navigation first took place, Old River that ends at the oil mill in Natchitoches was the first stream in use. One boat was lost below Montrose and another at Cypress. In Cane River I know of 2 boats that were lost — one opposite Front Street in Natchitoches and another at Live Oak plantation, six miles below town. One boat blew up its boilers, scalded to death Mr. H---, a planter living a few miles up. He died six days later. Mr. & Mrs. Fontenot were also burned by steam, but survived. This happened a mile below Monette ferry on the then Rosh plantation while loading cotton.

The boats used to take passengers & freight along the Red and expedition of cotton was made through them. There were landings all about, such as O.K., Lodi, Durand, Planters, and every farm was in fact a landing. From opposite Montgomery the planters were the Bernsteins, Dr. Jackson, the Currys. On Little River, Roper, Anthony and lower down some mullatoes owners of slaves. Then came Charleville, Duncan Cockfield, Judge Compere family; Compere's father came from Bordeaux with Hertzog & Roubieu. Another resident was E. Cockfield below Compere and also Louis (Gros) Rachal. Elyser Rachal and Pierre Brosset.

  Charles Bertrand,
  Cloutierville, 1933

Below: Foster & Glassett stern-wheel supply boat in front of Melrose Plantation, 29 December 1921.
Bottom: *W. T. Scovell* at Front Street.

Melrose Collection, NSU Archives

Giles W. Millspaugh, Jr., Collection, NSU Archives

Cane River home built in 1892 by Henry Stanley Stacy and wife Parthenia Wagley Stacy. Shown on the porch in 1912 are William Henry Stacy and wife Loretta Williams Stacy

Front Street at night, 1950s

Joe Dellmon Collection, NSU Archives

Christmas Festival fireworks, 1947

Joe Dellmon Collection, NSU Archives

Right: Ada Jack Carver, 1904
Far right: Ada Jack Carver, *Potpourri* editor, 1911
Below: Ada Jack Carver Snell and Mrs. Cammie Garrett Henry

George Williamson Collection, NSU Archives

Potpourri, 1911

Melrose Collection, NSU Archives

James Aswell autographing his novel *There's One in Every Town*

John S. Kyser Collection, NSU Archives

Ada Jack Carver and Lyle Saxon at Melrose Plantation, 1920s

Lyle Saxon

Melrose Collection, NSU Archives

Courtesy Joseph Henry, Sr.

Below: Captain Leopold Caspari
Top Right: Group of students with Uncle Snow at the gazebo, 1889
Lower Right: Children and students in front of the Normal School buildings

George Williamson Collection, NSU Archives

Tarleton Collection, NSU Archives

George Williamson Collection

House of Representatives, Session of 1884

My dear Julie,
... Tell Dr. Sheib & Judge Pierson that I received their letters They must excuse me, I am not able to answer for want of time; tell them I am not out of the woods yet. This Normal School has given me too much trouble. Last night the Senate Committee made a unanimous favorable report, and I think it will go through easy; but now comes the Governor who opposes it, he wants to keep us down to the 6000 dollars. I took our Senator awhile ago, and I gave the Governor a good talk; he says if other bills are cut down, he may approve ours. I have come to the conclusion to ask the Senate to pass it as it is and let him veto it if he wants. I am going in the senate now. L. Caspari

CANE RIVER COUNTRY Louisiana — 213

Colonel Thomas Duckett Boyd, president of the Louisiana State Normal School, photographed by A. D. Lytle, 1888

George Williamson Collection, NSU Archives

Beverly C. Caldwell, president of the Louisiana State Normal School, 1896-1908

George Williamson Collection, NSU Archives

The president's residence, State Normal School

George Williamson Collection, NSU Archives

... when I arrived in Natchitoches ... the impression of that snowy day in the old Southern town and the snow in the forest and upon the cotton fields was fantastic and beautiful and I cannot forget it.
Kate Chopin, 1900

801 Second Street

Courtesy Robert Smith, architect

The Mollie Campbell house

Melrose Collection, NSU Archives

In or around the year 1848, so the story goes, when Ulysses S. Grant was a Colonel in the United States Army and located at Camp Salubrity, which is about two miles north of the Town of Natchitoches on the Old Sabine Road, the second military road established between the Red River and the Sabine River, he became fascinated and fell in love with the beautiful and charming Mary Campbell, then one of the social Belles of Natchitoches. Colonel Grant was a sparkling young man of many social graces as well as great military ability. When the distinguished young colonel asked for her hand in marriage, Mary Campbell declined his offer of marriage and married Jerre Sullivan, a young man she was in love with. This preference to Jerre Sullivan, instead of the distinguished young colonel greatly changed the local history, for this young soldier later became the President of the United States. Mary Sullivan became the mother of Sheriff J. W. Freeman's first and second wives and the grandmother of Earl and Ashton Freeman.

James W. Jones, "The People and the Lands in the Red River Valley"

CANE RIVER COUNTRY Louisiana — 215

Joe Schelette, Natchitoches street sweeper, and his horse, Jack; 1931

Courtesy the City Bank, Natchitoches

Governor Newton Blanchard and James B. Aswell, Sr., president of the Louisiana State Normal School

George Williamson Collection, NSU Archives

James R. Hearron house [Historic District]

Courtesy B. A. Cohen

Kaffie-Moncla house [Historic District]

Courtesy B. A. Cohen

Ryan Horton, Jr., house [Historic District]
Courtesy B. A. Cohen

Robert Lucky house [Historic District]

Courtesy B. A. Cohen

First pecans of the season at the NSU Pecan Lab

Courtesy Dr. Arthur Allen, NSU

Tractor powered tree-shaker in position

Courtesy Dr. Arthur Allen, NSU

Courtesy Dr. Arthur Allen, NSU

Courtesy B. A. Cohen

The town of Marthaville was established upon the completion of the N.O.P. Railroad. It was established upon the lands of Capt. J. J. Rains, well-known through North Louisiana as one of its largest landed proprietors, and a gentleman of wealth and culture. The town, though small, is doing a good business, and it is surrounded by an extremely fertile country.... Mr. Rains has built a magnificent residence in the town, and this, together with similar edifices, gives it a splendid appearance.

F. H. Tompkins, *North Louisiana,* 1886

Courtesy B. A. Cohen

Courtesy B. A. Cohen

Top: tractor handling hardwood logs
Center: sawing logs in the mill
Left: stacks of sawed timbers

All bloomers worn by young ladies in athletic work must conform to patterns supplied or approved by the teacher of domestic art.
Louisiana State Normal School Catalog, 1916-1917

1918-1919 basketball team, LSNS

1931 basketball team, LSNC

John S. Kyser Collection, NSU Archives

Varsity baseball team, 1930

Photography class, 1902

George Williamson Collection, NSU Archives

For the study of photography there are two well-equipped dark rooms, a number of cameras and lenses of superior quality, and all necessary accessories. All these are used without charge by members of the photography class, but each student pays for the plates and printing paper for his own study.
Louisiana State Normal School Catalog, 1904

CANE RIVER COUNTRY Louisiana — 223

We've come to the Normal
  With one aim in view:
We're going to be teachers
  Before we get through.

We hear it in Chapel,
  We hear it at noon,
We're going to be teachers,
  And that pretty soon.

We're not to chew gum,
  Use slang, or wear paint,
But have prim deportment
  And act like a saint.

We'll go out in the State
  And models must be.
Everything that we do
  The children will see.

We must brace up, dear girls,
  Get good attitude,
Wear a smile that will stay
  And a look that's subdued.

We have the right feeling,
  The air it pervades.
We're sure to be teachers,
  And nice, prim old maids.

Potpourri, 1911

Normal College club girls, 1904

George Williamson Collection, NSU Archives

Diamond Jubilee, 1959

John S. Kyser Collection, NSU Archives

224 — CANE RIVER COUNTRY Louisiana

Courtesy B. A. Cohen

Patio in Ducournau Square [Historic District]

Patio of the Lemee house [Historic District]

Courtesy B. A. Cohen

United Methodist Church [Historic District]

Courtesy B. A. Cohen

Thomas P. Chaplin house [Historic District]

Courtesy B. A. Cohen

The Horse Soldiers: John Wayne and John Ford on filming location in Natchitoches Parish

Courtesy Guillet Photography

The Horse Soldiers: John Wayne

Courtesy Guillet Photography

The battle will be fought as numerous such savage engagements of the Civil War. It will have all the panoply of guidons and colors, bugle signals and the shoutings of orders. Horses and men will go down. Some men will get up and remount riderless horses. The ebb and flow of courage and death will eventually result in Marlowe, and what is left of his men, crossing the bridge and joining up with Secord and Gray's forces in hand-to-hand fighting, afoot and on horses with more and more sabre play as the attackers run out of ammunition, until they finally carry the field.

John Lee Mahin and Martin Rackin, *The Horse Soldiers.* Final script, 9 September 1958

First Baptist Church [Historic District]

Courtesy B. A. Cohen

Trinity Episcopal Church [Historic District]

Courtesy B. A. Cohen

I was nearly six years old when the final removal of the Indians took place, and I shall never forget the river banks in front of Natchitoches, lined with steamboats and the Front Street filled with gaudily-dressed Indians and their trappings.

They were a large population and their trade in pelts, tobacco, dried meats, tallow, beeswax, hides, beef cattle, baskets, and dressed skins was large and remunerative. After their deportation many business men left and houses were closed. It took time to fill the gap, and then the character of the commerce succeeding was altogether different, bringing in a new order of business men.

The stream of white immigration flowed on. In a few years, remarkably few, the Indian was forgotten. Some remained, and their language, once a required recommendation, together with Spanish and French, for a clerk or any young man in business, lapsed into desuetude. The last of the whites to speak it was a wealthy planter of Natchitoches Parish, but a few years dead, who kept some Indian families to hunt for him to his last days. Scrap books in old families yet contain Indian words with corresponding English translations, such as "we boys" all kept in that long ago.

J. H. Cosgrove

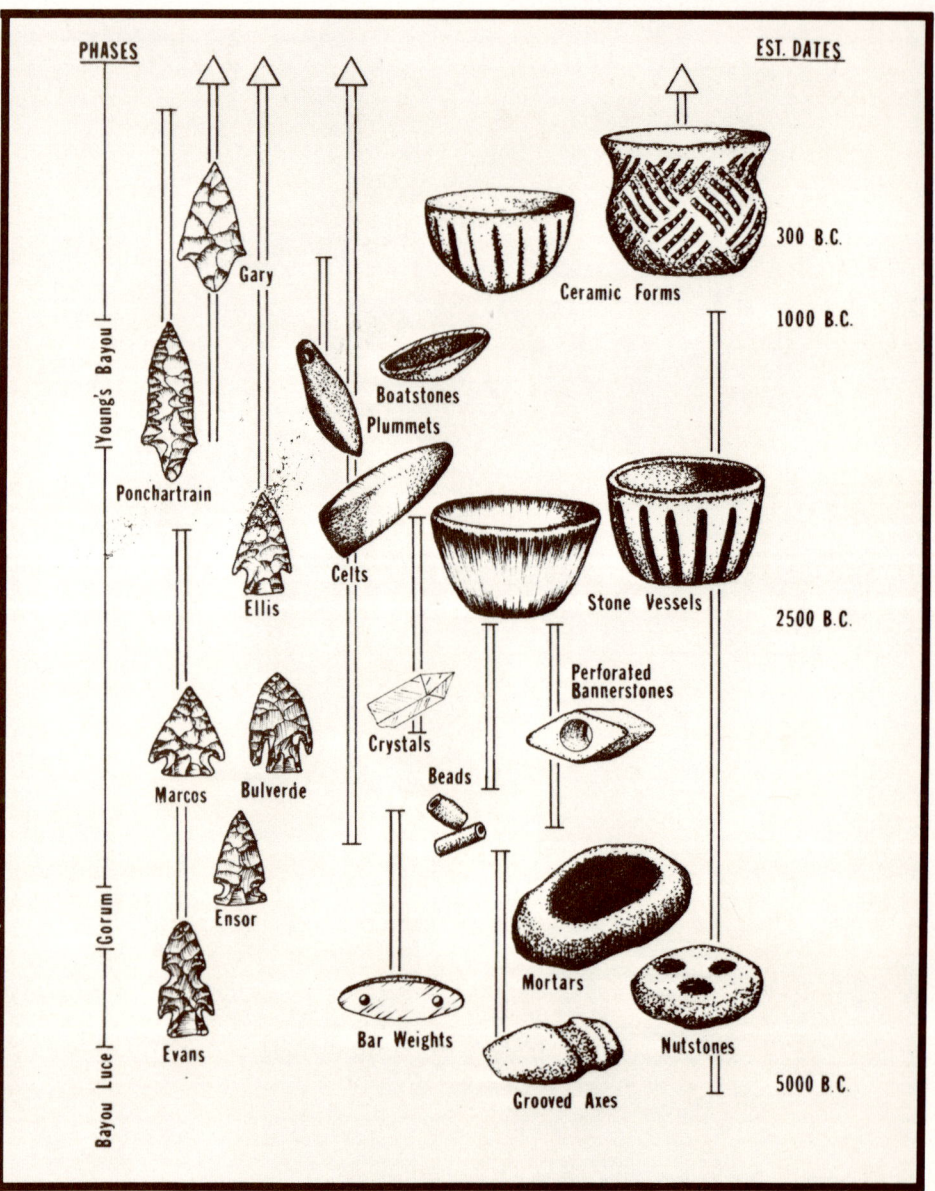

H. F. Gregory & H. K. Curry, Prehistory

John S. Kyser Collection, NSU Archives

Natchitoches Parish courthouse, Indian motif at front entrance [Historic District]

Northwestern State University students excavating an Indian site

Northwestern State University Photography

CANE RIVER COUNTRY Louisiana — 233

Mildred McCoy Collection, NSU Archives

Per Seyersted, A Kate Chopin Miscellany, *NSU Press, 1979*

Ah! drink, my soul, the splendor of
  the day;
Quaff from the golden goblet oft
  and deep.
Darkness will come again; too long
  'twill stay —
The everlasting night of dreamless
  sleep.
            Kate Chopin

Two portraits of Kate Chopin

Bayou Folk Museum.

Courtesy Mary Carolyn Roberts

CANE RIVER COUNTRY Louisiana — 235

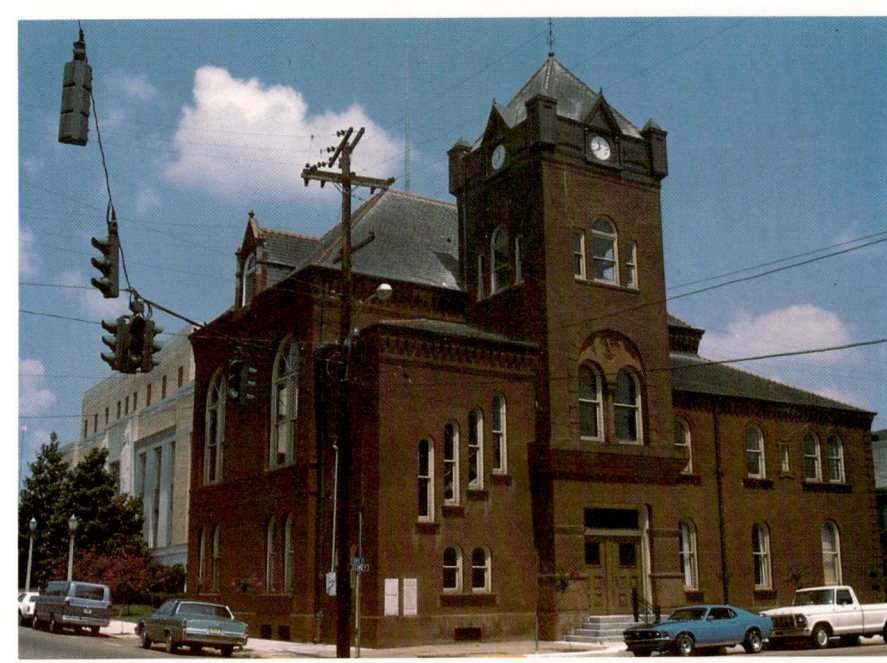

Right: old Natchitoches Parish court house. Below: Ducournau Square area of Front Street.

Courtesy B. A. Cohen

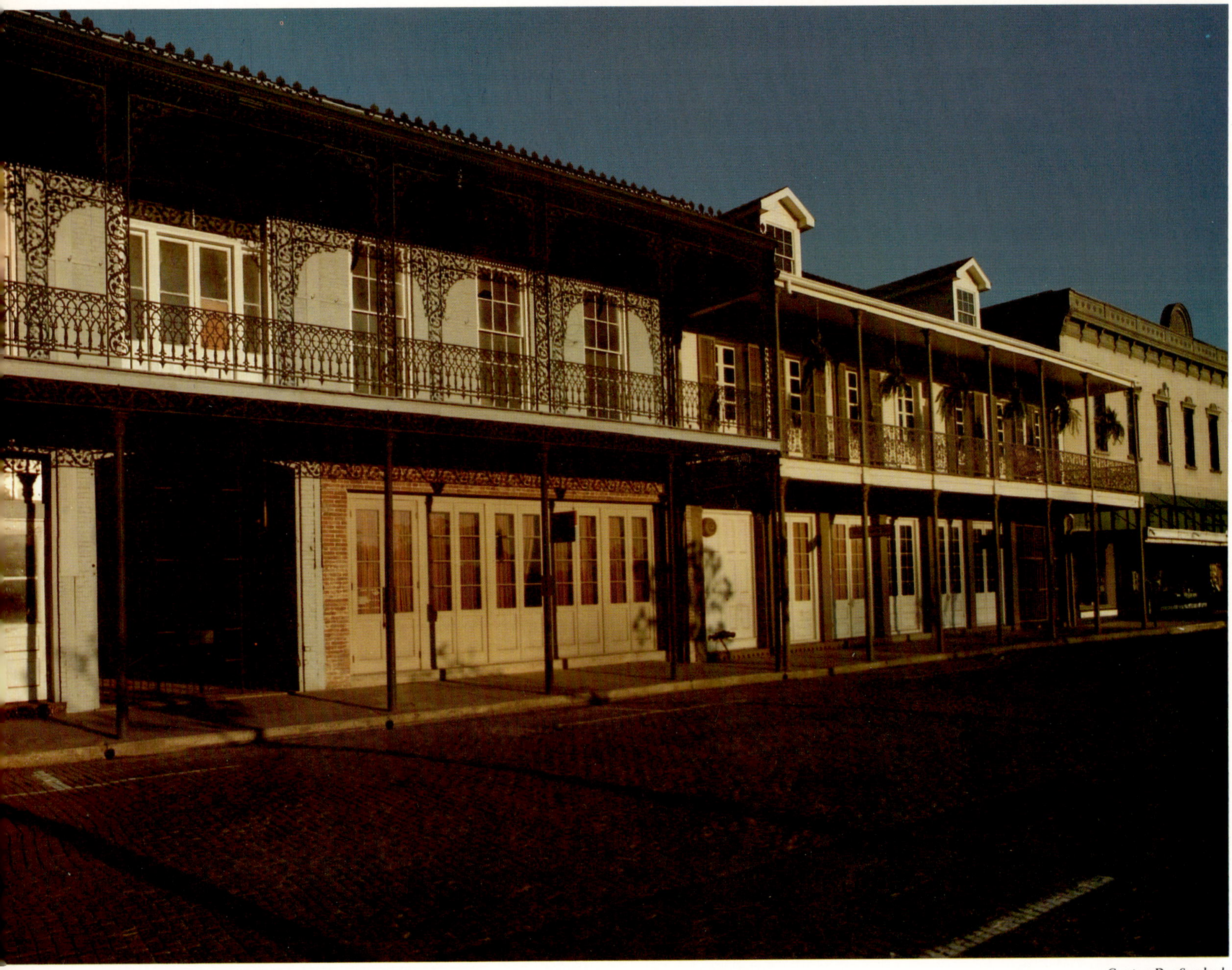

Courtesy Don Sepulvado

Courtesy B. A. Cohen

Left: spiral stairway.
Below: the Roque House now greets visitors on the Natchitoches riverfront.

Courtesy Don Sepulvado

CANE RIVER COUNTRY Louisiana — 237

Right: the Tante Huppé house. **Below:** the Henry Cook Taylor House.

© *Cane River Cuisine* photo by John C. Guillet

Courtesy B. A. Cohen

238 — CANE RIVER COUNTRY Louisiana

Courtesy Don MacKenzie

Courtesy Don Sepulvado

Courtesy B. A. Cohen

Top left: back of Melrose. Top right: African House, Melrose Plantation. Above: Melrose Plantation house.

CANE RIVER COUNTRY Louisiana — 239

Cherokee Plantation

Courtesy B. A. Cohen

Oakland Plantation

Courtesy B. A. Cohen

Laureate House

Courtesy B. A. Cohen

242 — CANE RIVER COUNTRY Louisiana

Beau Fort Plantation

Courtesy B. A. Cohen

The Levy House

Courtesy B. A. Cohen

244 — CANE RIVER COUNTRY Louisiana

Tante Huppé House.

Courtesy Mary Carolyn Roberts

Left: St. Augustine Church.
Below: Augustine Metoyer

Courtesy Guillet Photography

Courtesy NSU Archives

Courtesy Billie Sepulvado

Left: iron crosses in American Cemetery. Below: Immaculate Conception Catholic Church.

Courtesy B. A. Cohen

Lemee House

Courtesy B. A. Cohen

Ducournau Square Inc.

No. 8 Ducournau Square
Natchitoches, Louisiana
Owners:
Conna Glass Cloutier and P. E. Cloutier

When the present owners of Ducournau Square undertook to rescue a historic building that was totally without restoration, they embarked on an impressive pioneer project. Acquiring the Ducournau building in the Historic District in January 1977, they immediately started demolition of interior areas damaged by an earlier fire and began rebuilding, retaining much of the old while adding contemporary features. Shops were to occupy the lower floors and a town house, the upper story.

The Ducournau Building, in which the Town House is located, stands on a portion of an 1818 land grant made to Joseph Tauzin, who came from France in 1776 and married Marie Chamard in 1791. In 1819, Aaron Coe and Bernard Leonard bought the property. It is thought that the building was constructed between 1820 and 1847, for in 1820 Francois LaFonte purchased the property and carried on a business there until 1847, living upstairs over the first-floor business.

Lafonte left his interest in the business and building to his partner Alfred Daugerot. There followed a succession of owners: Daugerot's widow Adele (1852), F. Edward Cloutier and Pierre Lestan Prudhomme (1857), Victor Durand (1863), M.H. Carver (1869), John W. Cockerham (1878), and J.A. Ducournau (1881). The building's iron name plate came from a New Orleans store that Ducournau owned. Robert Smith and James Hearron acquired the property in 1974, the present owners in 1977.

Baker Printing

A Tour of the Town House

THE COURTYARD
Walking through wooden gates and down a carriageway, visitors find themselves in an Old World brick-paved courtyard. Behind dividing iron fencing, is a charming antique and gift shop, originally part of a carriage house. All the iron-work, including the fountain, was made at Starlight Plantation shop. The spikes atop the fencing are teeth from a mechanical cotton picker.

THE TOWN HOUSE
Stairs lead to a gallery and entrance to the Town House. In the foyer is an antique gold-leaf mirror, bought originally in New Orleans for Oaklawn Plantation house. The mirror rests on a marble base supported by rosewood piano legs.

From the foyer one views a great open area under a ceiling thirty feet high. A core stairway leads to balconies and third-floor bedrooms.

On the north wall are two original fireplaces. The building's original wood was used in reconstructing a more informal, contemporary design.

In the house are five armoires of different styles and periods, all from the Natchitoches area. A primitive armoire in the kitchen contrasts with the rare mahogany armoire (c. 1835) made by Dutreuil Bajon, Jr., a cabinet-maker who worked in New Orleans.

The Empire sideboard came from the Oaklawn Plantation; above it is a portrait of Marie Louise Elaiza Lambre (1812-1881), wife of Jacques Lestan Prudhomme (1801-1876).

The bedroom to the right of the foyer features a four-poster bed, and other local antique pieces. The dressing area shows a striking combination of hand-hewn beams and modern features.

The smaller area to the right of the living area is a guest study. Utility space and guest bath complete this level.

Four sets of French doors open onto a long gallery adorned with iron lace. Overlooking Cane River and downtown Natchitoches, one is reminded of a bygone lifestyle.

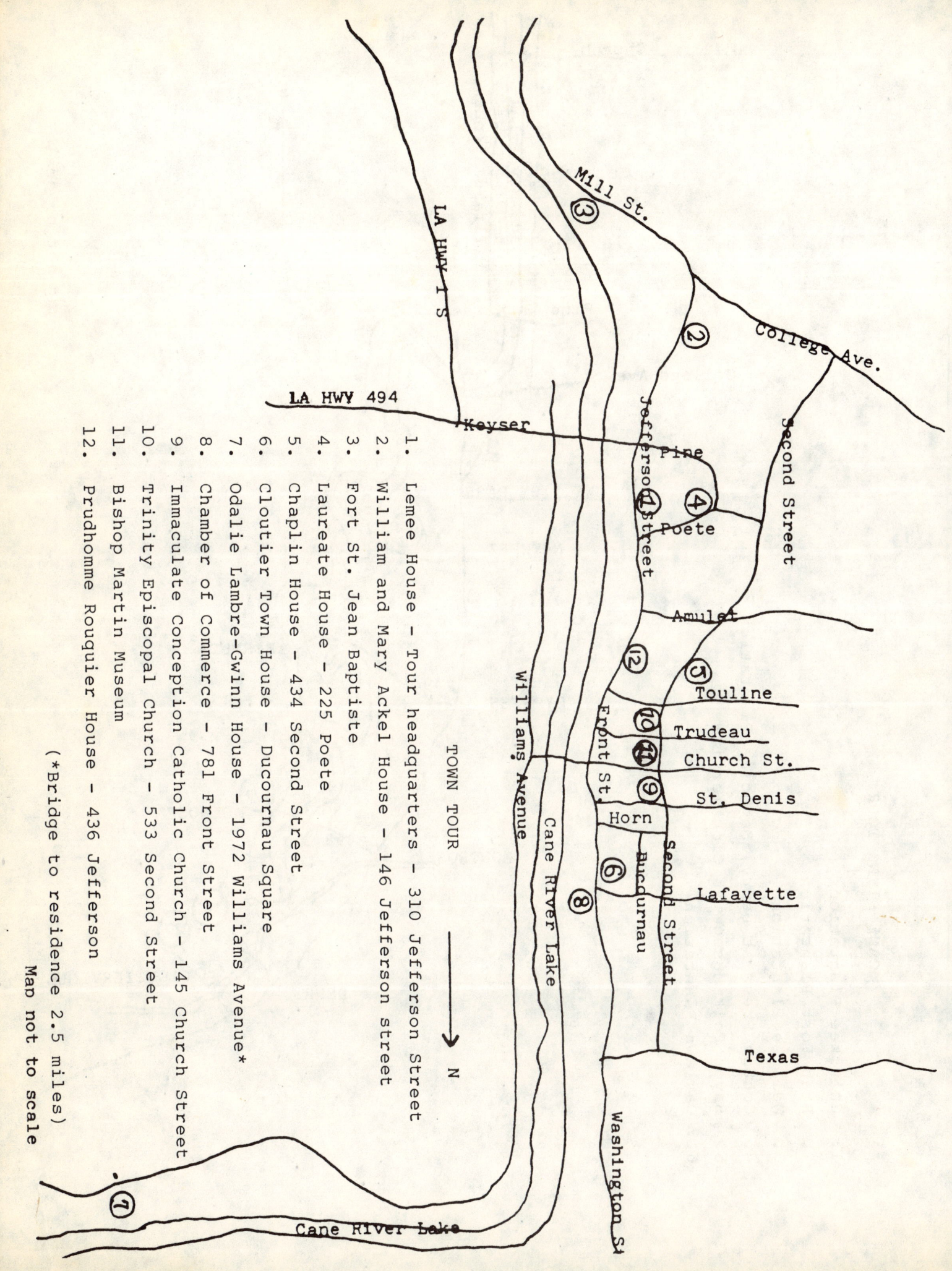

TOWN TOUR

1. Lemee House - Tour headquarters - 310 Jefferson Street
2. William and Mary Ackel House - 146 Jefferson street
3. Fort St. Jean Baptiste
4. Laureate House - 225 Poete
5. Chaplin House - 434 Second Street
6. Cloutier Town House - Ducournau Square
7. Odalie Lambre-Gwinn House - 1972 Williams Avenue*
8. Chamber of Commerce - 781 Front Street
9. Immaculate Conception Catholic Church - 145 Church Street
10. Trinity Episcopal Church - 533 Second Street
11. Bishop Martin Museum
12. Prudhomme Rouquier House - 436 Jefferson

(*Bridge to residence 2.5 miles)

Map not to scale

CANE RIVER TOUR

1. Cherokee Plantation
2. Beau Fort Plantation
3. Melrose Plantation
4. Cotton Press at Derry, Magnolia Plantation
5. Bayou Folk Museum at Cloutierville
6. Oaklawn Plantation

Map not to scale

The Lemee House

310 Jefferson Street
Natchitoches, Louisiana

Shortly after the Louisiana Purchase, all previously held land grants were verified by the United States government, and this property was listed in a document, now held by Mr. Robert DeBlieux, as belonging to Athanase de Mezieres, son-in-law of St. Denis. He deeded it to Natalie de Mezieres, F.W.C., c. 1811. Finally it was purchased by Soldini, one of the Italian contractors who came to Natchitoches in the early nineteenth century. Soldini evidently built the house for himself as he included several items not in any other house they built. Note the five-panel effect of the brickwork on the front, each panel centered by a window or a door and the unique locking system of large metal hooks and eyes. Note the "cradle" roof on the back, the only roof so-built in the United States, but common along the Mediterranean coasts, where the little upswing at the eaves diverted and divided the force of the strong wind and prevented roofing's being torn off in storms.

Another special item was the brick floored and walled basement, evidently to preserve Italian sausages and keep Italian wine cool. Note also the cistern, half in the cellar and half out so that water could be caught during rains but women did not have to get wet to get water into the kitchen. Note that there were originally three fanlights over the three doors on the patio.

In 1849 the house was bought by Alexis Lemee to use as a house and a bank building for his employers, the Union Bank of New Orleans. There is a tradition — not authenticated — that during its use as such, a tunnel extended from the east wall of the basement to the river so that gold could be transferred safely to the bank. When the bank was discontinued, Lemee bought the building and continued to live in it.

It changed hands repeatedly during the next century. Finally in 1940 a committee sent here on the Historic Homes Survey was intrigued by the house and its history. The architect took steps toward buying it. This prompted women of the town to prevail upon the City Council to buy it for the city. With ownership remaining municipal, the women pledged to restore it, furnish it, and use it as a Women's Club House. This proved a very expensive and onerous job but has been accomplished.

BAKER PRINTING & OFFICE SUPPLY

A Tour of the House

Only the south wall is completely new; the inside walls were treated and reinforced. The ceilings are original cypress, as are the dining room fireplace and the mantel in the hall. All door and window frames with their "picture-frame" appearance are also original, as is much of the glass.

The furnishings are gifts of individuals or groups, each piece honoring some Natchitoches woman. Some are purchases of the Association. To itemize is impossible.

HALL

The painting is of Mrs. Michael Boyce, nee Roubieu, daughter-in-law of the man for whom Boyce is named. The mirror over the mantel once framed a portrait of the Mr. Caspari for whom Caspari Hall is named. The portrait was given to the Hall, the old frame with mirror to the Lemee House.

The woman in her wedding dress, in picture over the tilt-top table, is Lillie Sompayrac Ducournau (Mrs. J. A.), the great granddaughter of Alexis Lemee. Her wedding reception was held in this house. Note the mahogany Empire couch, the English hurricane lamps, round French table, Victorian fireside chair, Seth Thomas clock (c. 1805).

CLUBROOM

The most important item in this room is the map on the east wall, first map of the area, drawn by a French engineer, J. F. Broutin in 1792. On the west wall is a map of the Presidio de Los Adaes, easternmost fort of the Spanish holdings. The original is in the British Museum in London. Also on this wall is an historical map of Louisiana, lent by Dr. John S. Kyser.

Note the Napoleonic desk in the east corner. It was given by a group of New Orleans women (among whom was Dorothy Dix) and has a secret drawer.

DINING ROOM

Note rosewood table, crystal candelabrum, silver tray, punch bowl, and coffee urn.

PATIO

The Rena Phillips Fountain is noteworthy for the pattern of frogs and turtles in its ironwork.

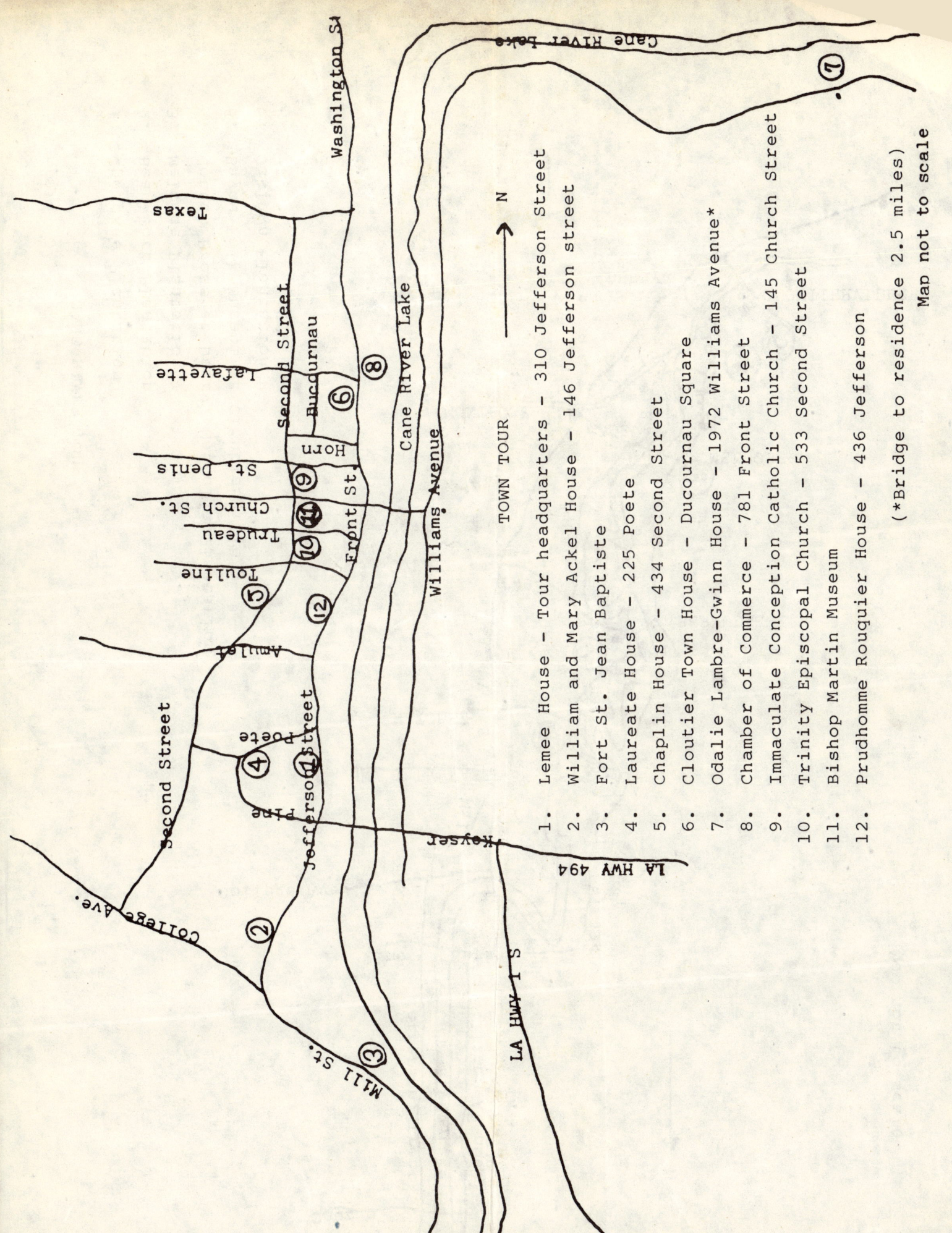

CANE RIVER TOUR

1. Cherokee Plantation
2. Beau Fort Plantation
3. Melrose Plantation
4. Cotton Press at Derry, Magnolia Plantation
5. Bayou Folk Museum at Cloutierville
6. Oaklawn Plantation

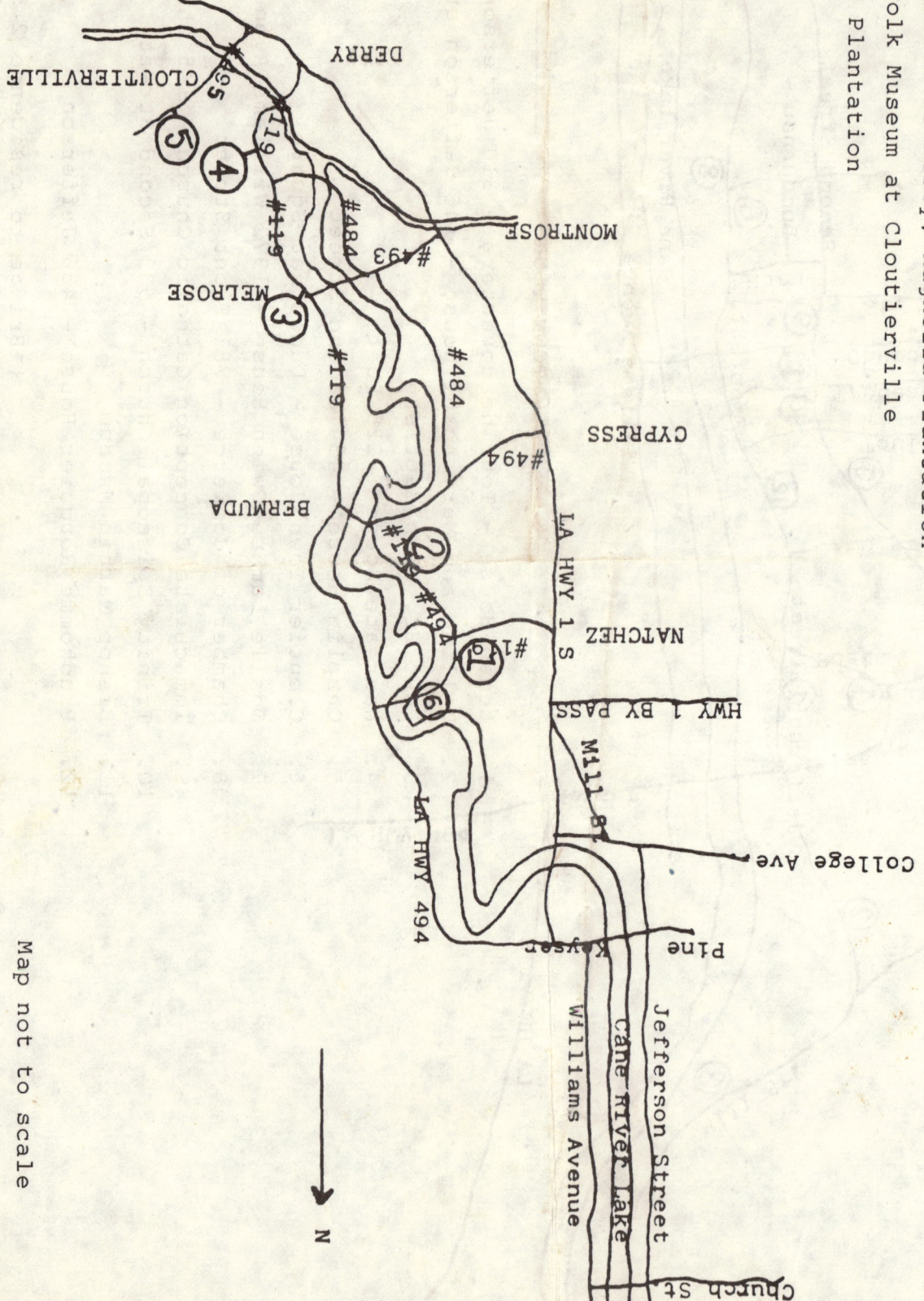

Map not to scale

Beau Fort Plantation Home

Bermuda, Louisiana
Owner: Association for the Preservation
of Historic Natchitoches

Beau Fort, formerly the home of Mrs. C. Vernon Cloutier, is a one and one-half story cottage-type building, with three French doors opening onto an 84-foot front gallery. Of Creole architecture, the home lies at the head of an avenue of live oaks and is surrounded by beautifully landscaped gardens.

Beau Fort was built about 1790 for Louis Barthelemy Rachal and his wife on land which he had received in a Spanish grant accorded by Baron de Carondelet. In 1834 the plantation was purchased by Narcisse Prudhomme, and remained in that family until 1928, when it became Cloutier property.

Original work on the plantation residence was crudely done by unskilled slave labor. Walls were constructed of hand-hewn cypress timbers and an adobe-like mixture of mud, deer hair, and Spanish moss. Still in evidence are the original floors and hardware. Architects marvel that the attic beams are solid pieces going the length of the house.

The interior architecture of Beau Fort is unusual in that there is not a single wall that goes all the way through from front to back, or from end to end. Though there is no hall, all rooms have privacy, yet easy access. When Beau Fort was remodeled, a door was cut from the Stranger's Room to the study, smaller than other doors because of the old studding.

Seeing the home now in its entirety with its charm and distinction, one would not suspect the state of disrepair the old building had fallen into before Mrs. Cloutier and the late Mr. Cloutier decided in 1948 to restore it. Using pieces of massive furniture discovered in attics, old family portraits that she rescued, fine old French Creole furnishings from the Payne, Prudhomme, Blanchard, Rouquier, and Williams families, Mrs. Cloutier succeeded in creating a splendid harmony in each room. More recent additions include Oriental rugs and ornaments dating back to the Ming Dynasty. The result is an elegant but wonderfully livable home.

An exceptionally beautiful enclosed courtyard features a patio of old brick, and an unusual brick wall with oval-shaped iron grillwork air vents.

Beau Fort's name, suggested by Francois Mignon, comes from the tradition that the house is situated on the site of one of the first forts in the area. In 1976, Beau Fort was placed on the U.S. Department of Interior's National Register of Historic Places.

In 1980, Mrs. Cloutier willed Beau Fort to the Association for the Preservation of Historic Natchitoches to operate as a museum.

A Tour of the House

LIVING ROOM

Walnut Victorian sofa. Drop-leaf card table of crotch mahogany, early Creole. English rosewood chest, 1820. Vieux Paris porcelain lamps. Sconces, English jets, of Waterford crystal and brass.
Crystal hurricane shades, 1830. Sugar bowl, of darker coin silver, c. 1790, gift to Marianne Rouquier. Lap-desk table from Payne family. Ming Dynasty celadon bowl. Petit point pictures from Vienna.

LIBRARY

All furniture of the Louisiana Creole Period. Color scheme: red, white, and blue. Wallpaper of plantation scenes, made especially for the library. Curtains and upholstery woven by the Cloutiers.
Portrait of Charles Vernon Cloutier (1899-1962) by Delano Cooper.
Gentleman's plantation desk of rosewood, lined with Circassian walnut, 1790. Sofa and wing chair of Napoleonic era. Man's duchet, a shaving dresser, c. 1820; duchesse in the Stranger's Room a companion piece.
Lowestoft bowl 200 years old. Crest and coats of arms made by heraldist of Louvre Museum.

DINING ROOM

All furniture Creole Louisiana. Old Plauche armoire converted into china cabinet. Chairs by Seignouret of New Orleans, 1830-1840. Seat covers, needlepoint from Austria, done by Mrs. Cloutier.
Punkah, installed when house was built.

STRANGER'S ROOM

Oldest bed in house, constructed in 1790, its posts hand-carved in a pineapple and acanthus leaf pattern. Pie crust table from Payne family. Victorian fan vases. Miniature hats on mantel, French Tole.

GUEST BEDROOM

Armoire and bed, early Louisiana period. Italian chandelier.

MASTER BEDROOM and EXTRA BEDROOM

Identical sets of Mallard mahogany Creole furniture, 1840.

Melrose Plantation Homes
Melrose, Louisiana

The Buildings

THE BIG HOUSE (1833): Early Louisiana type plantation home. It was begun by Louis Metoyer, completed by his son. The Henrys added the *garconnieres*.

YUCCA (c. 1796): The original colonial residence. The sills and uprights are of virgin cypress, the walls of mud mixed with moss and deer hair. Yucca has housed more of America's notable authors and historians than any other single residence in the South.

THE AFRICAN HOUSE (c. 1800): The slave-fort and provision house. Its lower story is of brick baked on the place, while the upper story is fashioned from thick hand-hewn cypress slabs. The walls of the upper story are entirely covered with Clementine Hunter creations.

THE WEAVING HOUSE: Cabin restored in 1973 in memory of Mrs. Nettie Hubier Russell by her daughter.

THE BINDERY
THE WRITER'S CABIN

GHANA: Cabin that originated, probably, on Metoyer land. It is generally believed to be almost as old as the other colonial buildings.

Owner: Association of Natchitoches Women for the Preservation of Historic Natchitoches. Title conveyed by Southdown Land Company in 1971.

THE METOYER FAMILY AT MELROSE

The threads of the Melrose story — a legend based on fact — go back to Marie Therese Coincoin, a slave born (in 1742) into the household of St. Denis, first Commandant of the post at Natchitoches. She lived to become the matriarch of a family of fourteen children — four black and ten of Franco-African blood — and the founder of an agricultural dynasty and of a unique colony of people. Her son Augustin is the "Grandpere" to whom Cane River descendants trace their ancestry, and so to Marie Therese.

After the deaths of St. Denis and his widow, Marie Therese and her mulatto children were sold (1776-1780) to Thomas Pierre Metoyer, a Frenchman. All evidence points to Metoyer as the father of her Franco-African children. In 1780 Metoyer freed her, and eventually he freed all her enslaved mulatto children.

Metoyer deeded to Marie Therese a small grant of land. A larger grant on Old River was made to her in the name of the Spanish King. And in 1796, her son Louis obtained a large grant, the present Melrose Plantation, which, presumably, Marie Therese held for Louis until he was free and thereby permitted to own property. Other sons were established on their own tracts.

Among other sterling attributes, Marie Therese was endowed with unusual energy and intelligence. This resourceful woman, her sons, and her slaves worked valiantly, clearing the land, cultivating tobacco, corn, and other crops, raising cattle, to achieve a successful plantation operation.

Marie Therese had not forgotten her black children. This remarkable woman worked to purchase the freedom of two of her black children and at least one of her grandchildren. She lived past the age of 73, to see her grandchildren prosperous and living good lives.

THE HENRY YEARS AT MELROSE

The second part of the story of Melrose revolves around another remarkable woman, Cammie Garrett Henry, wife of John Hampton Henry. When the Henrys moved to Melrose in 1898, "Miss Cammie" was brimming over with energy and enthusiasm that centered on bringing Melrose back to its former beauty and making it a repository of local arts and crafts, history, and legend.

It was a fabulous program Miss Cammie laid out for herself — maintaining an extensive household, replanting and extending the Melrose gardens, rescuing the colonial buildings, accumulating a library, reviving local handicrafts. Less fortunate neighbors of color had to be looked after. Journals of old days, portraits, heirlooms, had to be preserved. A collection of scrapbooks had to be increased.

The plantation became a Mecca for artists and writers—Roark Bradford, Rachel Field, Rose Franken, William Spratling, Harnett Kane, Gwen Bristow, Alberta Kinsey, among others. Here Lyle Saxon wrote his *Children of Strangers*. Here Clementine Hunter, Louisiana's most celebrated primitive artist, worked and received encouragement to paint her scenes of plantation life. Here, also, lived Francois Mignon, author of *Plantation Memo*, who arrived for a six-week visit and stayed for thirty-two years. After Mrs. Henry's death, Mignon furthered the cultivation of the gardens and helped foster the arts and crafts to which she had devoted her life.

Cherokee Plantation Home

Natchez, Louisiana
Owners:
Mr. and Mrs. William Nolan

Cherokee is part of a Spanish land grant issued to Philippe Frederique and Jacques Faure in 1795. The house dates back to some years before 1839 when Emile Sompayrac purchased the plantation from his father-in-law Narcisse Prud'homme and altered the house for his wife Clarisse. In that same year, the famous Bossier-Gaiennie duel was fought at the rear of the plantation.

After Emile's death in 1878, parcels of the property were sold, and in 1891 the remainder was bought by Robert Calvert Murphy.

Built of "bousillage" (mud mixed with moss and deer hair), the raised-type construction has the original six fireplaces and tall folding doors of "faux bois" (the grain painted on the wood). Doors of this type are used throughout the house. All the wide-board floors are original, as are the windows and doors with panes of hand-blown glass, and a large number of the locks and pieces of hardware.

There are porches on three sides of the house. Eighteen columns of hand-hewn cypress extend from porch level to the eaves. The entire skeletal structure of the building, the massive sills, the floor beams, the ceiling beams and the studding are hand-hewn cypress.

Now the property of Mr. and Mrs. William Nolan of El Dorado, Ark., granddaughter of the first Murphy to own the house, Cherokee has been restored by the owners. Many pieces of the furniture have been used in the house since 1891.

A Tour of the House

LIVING ROOM

Impressive mahogany Empire secretary, probably Southern-made c. 1850. Upright piano with classic pressed copper insets made in Boston, mid-19th century. Low table with painted top attributed to Angelica Kaufmann, late 18th century artist, one of the founders of the Royal Academy.

Large pair of Audubon bird prints printed in 1860. Small white marble 18th century French clock on mantel. 1833 French pole fire screen. Antique Tabriz rug.

Portrait of Robert Calvert Murphy at eighty-seven years of age.

RIGHT FRONT BEDROOM
(Once "stranger's room," later used as Marston Post Office)

Handmade armoire almost ten feet high, said to have been made by slaves on Cane River. Chest from old Natchitoches home. Wallpaper of French Toile de Jouy is balloon design. Interesting circular French night table.

RED BATHROOM
(Formerly a bedroom)

Excellent example of mid-19th century hanging oil lamp in hobnail cranberry glass. Painted German cabinet, late 19th century. 1820 French bidet. Examples of Mary Gregory glassware on mantel shelf.

GUEST BEDROOM
(Once served as pantry)

Victorian bedroom set from Murphy family. Note trap door leading to cellar. Handwoven coverlet made about 1800 by Mrs. Nolan's great-great-grandmother.

DINING ROOM

Wall covering of cotton Chaldean print in indigo blue. Original punkah made on the plantation. Table from old Mississippi home. Ironstone tureen and china. Buffet from Murphy family. Petticoat table from New Orleans. Family tree made by oldest daughter of R. C. Murphy. French clock called a "Wag-on-the-Wall."

KITCHEN

Note old plantation safe which belonged to Prud'homme family. Caboose light over the breakfast table.

LEFT BACK BEDROOM

Bed and dresser from Murphy family. Handwoven coverlet in family for over 200 years, made by Agnes Keesse, great-grandmother of R. C. Murphy, in 1740. Armoire from the mountains of Switzerland, called a Wedding Chest, hand-painted primitive designs. Note Covered Wagon chair.

BACK BATHROOM and HALL

Note very old French doll and the little dolls with German china heads. A section of hall has been left unfinished to show original construction.

LARGE BEDROOM

Louisiana style furniture from New Orleans. Plantation bed. Spool sewing cabinet. Interesting hanging oil lamp, which has a device for raising and lowering.

Oak Lawn Plantation

Courtesy B. A. Cohen

Tauzin-Wells House

Courtesy B. A. Cohen